LOL

LAUGHING OUT LOUD? NO
LITTLE OLD LADY? NO

IT'S LOSER - ON - LOSER

JAMES MARSH STERNBERG
DANNY KLEINMAN

authorHOUSE

AuthorHouse™
1663 Liberty Drive
Bloomington, IN 47403
www.authorhouse.com
Phone: 833-262-8899

Published by AuthorHouse 08/27/2021

ISBN: 978-1-6655-3623-3 (sc)
ISBN: 978-1-6655-3624-0 (e)

Print information available on the last page.

Any people depicted in stock imagery provided by Getty Images are models,
and such images are being used for illustrative purposes only.
Certain stock imagery © Getty Images.

This book is printed on acid-free paper.

CONTENTS

Chapter 3. Ruffing Problems by Danny Kleinman

DEDICATION

To Bridge Hall of Famer

FRED

HAMILTON

Thanks Freddy, for the joy of all our wins together, and the suffering
of the losses

JMS

"And here's to you,

Mrs. GUGGENHEIM!

Simon loves you more than you will know, wo–wo–wo!"

DK

ACKNOWLEDGMENTS

This book would not have been possible without the help of several friends. Frank Stewart, Michael Lawrence, Anne Lund, and Eddie Kantar all kindly provided suggestions for material for the book.

We are forever indebted to Alan Brody, Norman Gore, Dick Recht, Norbert Jay, and the late Bernie Chazen, without whose guidance and teaching we could not have achieved whatever success we have had in bridge.

And of course, Jim wants to thank Vickie Lee Bader, whose love and patience helped guide him thru the many hours of this endeavor.

James Marsh Sternberg, MD   Danny Kleinman, Psephologist

Palm Beach Gardens, FL   Los Angeles, CA

INTRODUCTION TO LOL 😆

Just what is LOL? Yes, a common abbreviation for Laughing Out Loud, and often used to refer to a Little Old Lady, but in bridge it means a Loser-On-Loser play. At times a declarer can improve his/her situation by playing a losing card from one hand on a loser in a different suit from the hand opposite. This occurs when a player has a loser in two suits but can arrange to lose them both on one trick, thereby reducing the number of losers from two to one. Often this looks like a Ruff-and-Sluff play, but instead of ruffing, declarer or dummy discards a loser in each hand. When and why would one do this?

This technique has many uses. One example is to keep the 'Danger' hand off lead. Often in the end game it serves as the exit in assisting the process of elimination and placing the lead in the hand of the desired opponent for an endplay. The advantage of this procedure is that declarer divests himself of two losers while simultaneously placing the lead in the desired quarter.

Another example is for the purpose of severing communication between the defending hands, making oneself void of the suit where the communication exists. The purpose of this play is usually to prevent one defender from giving the other a ruff, and has become known as the Scissors Coup. Another example is when in a Moysian fit, a 4/3 trump fit, and declarer needs to discard rather than ruff in the long, the 4-card trump holding. Or the opponents may be threatening a trump promotion. Rather than ruffing, discard a loser that you would have lost later anyhow.

This book is divided into chapters along the above lines but of course there is overlap; some hands could be in more than one chapter. All four hands are shown. Try covering the East-West hands first and solve the problem before viewing the entire deal; you have a big clue. I think you will find the deals interesting and instructive and recognize situations from your own previous experiences. Have fun. Sure, LOL.

PRELUDE

A Loser-on-Loser play, LOL, is a type of declarer play, usually in trump contracts, where the declarer discards a losing card, one that is bound to be given up anyway, on an opponent's winner instead of ruffing.

When might this be appropriate? An LOL play occurs when for example, you have a loser in two suits but can arrange to lose them both on one trick, thereby cutting the number of losers from two to one.

Often this situation will look like a Ruff-Sluff play, but instead of ruffing, you or the dummy pitch a loser on the led suit and then a second loser in another suit in the other hand, instead of ruffing.

Although you may lose a trick you could win, it may be advantageous to lose that trick in order to discard a loser in another suit. Why and when might this be?

One example is both the declarer and dummy have a club loser which would enable the defenders to communicate, proving fatal to your contract, by a ruff or allowing a danger hand to obtain the lead.

But instead of ruffing a trick, declarer discards a club from one hand or the other, voiding that hand and breaking the communication

LOL technique can be executed for the following goals.

1. Avoiding an opponent having the opportunity to ruff.
2. To keep the lead in the 'safe', rather than the 'danger' hand.
3. To maintain trump control, especially in 4-3 fits.
4. When preparing an endplay.
5. To rectify the count for a subsequent squeeze play.

The breaking of the communication between the opponents' hands with a LOL play is referred to as a Scissors Coup. This may be seen in any of the above situations.

We will try to look at these in the coming chapters.

DANNY'S AUTOBIOGRAPHICAL NOTE

In the mid-1960s, after a hard day's work and dinner at a nearby restaurant, I would adjourn to The Office (to use Bob Hamman's name for it), aka the Los Angeles Bridge Club, which Albert Okuneff (inventor of the "Western Cue Bid" that asked partner to bid 3NT with a stopper) operated. It was in a building bordered by Melrose Avenue and Santa Monica Boulevard as they merged just east of Doheny Drive in West Hollywood.

In one corner of the "Open Room" where Al's other patrons gathered lay a table that was reserved for a rotating group of players who met nightly for team-of-four play at IMPs. We would cut for teams, four red cards versus four black cards. Each team would arrange its own pairings. We would play 8-board matches for a dollar an IMP, with a 4-IMP bonus for winning the match and a 35-IMP limit. Then we'd cut for teams anew. A small room off to the side served as the "Closed Room" to which four of us, perhaps with a kibitzer or two in tow, adjourned.

Sometimes we would have nine participants, in which case a different member of our loose group would be consigned to kibitzing the match. I will name only the participants whose skills and character I most respect. You may recognize four who were world class: Bob Hamman, Meyer Schleifer, Eddie Kantar and (when he drove in from San Bernardino) Marshall Miles.

Conspicuously absent were Alfred Sheinwold, who had an office in the building, and Barry Crane, who played duplicate at ACBL tournaments but played only high-stakes gin rummy at rubber bridge clubs. Also absent were women players, except for two, Stella Rebner and Fran Tsacnaris (or "Sackarackis" as she mockingly called herself). They were talented enough to play in the strongest company.

Of the others, I shall mention only two, of whom my memories are fondest: Bill McWilliams and Eliot Bean.

Few bridge books mention perhaps the most vital bridge skills: *social and psychological* skills. The most conspicuous exception is S.J. Simon's *Why You Lose at Bridge*. The biggest tragedy of my bridge career came in 1948, when Simon died, years before I heard of him or read his books. In this book, I shall pay homage to my bridge idol by using his fearsome foursome, Mrs. Guggenheim, Futile Willie, Mr. Smug and the Unlucky Expert, as dramatis personae in the deals, and I'll add a few characters of my own. I hope this will inspire you to read Simon's books.

The usual social skills in bridge are in attracting and keeping good partners, and increasingly, acquiring money enough to hire the many whose sessions are for sale. A sadly overlooked social skill is negotiating partnership agreements. That is my second-best social skill, and it is meager indeed. All too often I am outstubborned by partners.

However, it was my best social skill that allowed me to survive and thrive in the "Rough and Tumble" team games at The Office. That was to arrange partnerships within my team. The players I have named were not the only participants. I have named eight, but seldom if ever were all nine of us present at the same time. Almost always, there were one or two weaker players among us: *pigeons*, as we often called them. Bob Hamman claimed *all* bridge players were his pigeons.

I won't claim to be a better bridge player than Bob, but I am a better ornithologist. Bob was happy to play with Eddie Kantar (who wouldn't be?) but not so happy to play with pigeons. My strategy at Rough and Tumble Teams was to strengthen what would otherwise be the weakest pair on my team. That was not always the pair with the weakest player, it was the pair with the *most difficult partner*. When Stella (whose instinctive card play compared favorably with anybody's but Meyer's) was among us, it was she.

As soon as I knew my teammates, I volunteered to play with the most difficult. When we had a pigeon on our team, he was thrilled to be chosen first, and the two strong players were delighted to play with each other.

One evening, I cut Bob, Eddie and Meyer as my teammates against a record *four* pigeons. It was like playing on the 1926 Yankees with Babe Ruth, Lou Gehrig and Tony Lazzeri. I thought I was Miller Huggins and tried to arrange the lineup. Choose the right one and we sweep the World Series in four games. Choose the second-best lineup and we win in six. Choose the worst and we lose to Alexander's Ragtag Band.

Bob outstubborned me. I will never let him forget the result.

In the deals that follow, imagine yourself as South in circumstances like mine in 1966 or so, declaring contracts at IMPs, where overtricks and undoubled undertricks count for little. Making your contract is virtually your only concern. If you can, cover the East-West hands with a strip of paper or cardboard and choose your plays. Then see how the South in the Open Room messed up and the South in the Closed Room did better.

Danny Kleinman

CHAPTER ONE

THE SCISSORS COUP

What is a Scissors Coup? The Encyclopedia Of Bridge defines it as "a play aimed at cutting the opponents' communication,... (sometimes called less descriptively the 'coup without a name')."

Since it's actually a play that deprives defenders of *transportation* between hands, Danny calls it a Car Coup. A different coup, ducking a trick you must lose early, to deprive defenders of information about the suit, such as the completion of a count signal, he calls a Phone Coup.

Goren's book "On Play and Defense," 1974, described the Scissors Coup "to sever communication between defending hands, make yourself void of the suit where the connection exists." He goes on to say "it is sometimes good play for the declarer to lead a suit with no other object than to sever the defenders' communication in this suit. The usual purpose of this play.....is to prevent a ruff by the defenders."

As we will see as we travel thru this book, this play has other purposes besides preventing a ruff. Avoidance plays, danger hands, trump management, preparing and executing an endplay are common other uses of the Scissors Coup, and all involve, in one way or another a Loser – On – Loser play.

There is as we said considerable overlap between chapters. Let's start with a few miscellaneous scissors coups and then try to break some hands into chapters. OK, let's go!

DEAL 1. SCISSORS COUP

```
                    ♠ 7 5 4
                    ♡ K J 8 7
                    ◇ 5 4
                    ♣ A K J 3
    ♠ Q J 9                        ♠ A K 10 6 3
    ♡ void                         ♡ A 4 3 2
    ◇ 10 9 6 2                     ◇ 8 7 3
    ♣ Q 10 8 7 6 5                 ♣ 2
                    ♠ 8 2
                    ♡ Q 10 9 6 5
                    ◇ A K Q J
                    ♣ 9 4
```

North opened 1♣ and East overcalled 1♠. South bid 2♡ and reached 4♡ after North raised hearts. West led the ♠Q.

East overtook with the ♠K and returned a club. His plan was to win the first trump and having kept an entry to West's hand, to put him in and get a club ruff.

Seeing only three fast losers, declarer started trumps. East won the heart ace and led to West's spade jack. When West returned a club for East to ruff, declarer was down one.

How did the declarer in the other room overcome this good defense?

In the other room, after winning the club return, declarer clearly saw the problem. To counter this, he started the diamonds, discarding spades from dummy. East ruffed the fourth diamond, but declarer no longer had a spade loser.

A fair trade. But more important was that he had severed the defenders' link. East could no longer reach West for a club ruff.

Making four hearts, losing only one spade and two trump tricks.

DEAL 2. PASS THE SCISSORS PLEASE

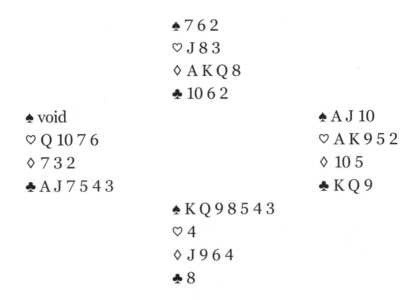

♠ 7 6 2
♡ J 8 3
♢ A K Q 8
♣ 10 6 2

♠ void
♡ Q 10 7 6
♢ 7 3 2
♣ A J 7 5 4 3

♠ A J 10
♡ A K 9 5 2
♢ 10 5
♣ K Q 9

♠ K Q 9 8 5 4 3
♡ 4
♢ J 9 6 4
♣ 8

East opened 1♡ and South bid 3♠. West raised to 4♡, North to 4♠ and East's double ended the auction. West led a low heart to East's king. Declarer ruffed the heart continuation.

Declarer led a diamond to dummy to start the trumps. East played the ten, declarer won as West showed out. Declarer led another diamond to dummy for another trump play. This time East took his ace and led a club. West won and gave East a diamond ruff. Down one, doubled. Ouch.

"Partner, couldn't you see this coming and have avoided it," asked North?

How could South have prevented the ruff and made his doubled contract?

In the other room, declarer foresaw the potential problem. After winning the first trump, he led a club himself. When he later went to dummy with a diamond, East could no longer reach West.

The Scissors Coup strikes again! Making four spades doubled.

DEAL 3. A SIMILAR SITUATION

```
                    ♠ 10 5
                    ♡ 7 5 3
                    ◊ Q 10 9 2
                    ♣ A K Q 4
    ♠ 9 4                         ♠ A J 8
    ♡ 10 8 4 2                    ♡ A J 9 6
    ◊ K 7 6 3                     ◊ A J 8 5
    ♣ 7 6 5                       ♣ J 2
                    ♠ K Q 7 6 3 2
                    ♡ K Q
                    ◊ 4
                    ♣ 10 9 8 3
```

East opened 1NT, 15-17 HCP and South overcalled 2♠. North invited game bidding 2NT and South bid 4♠. West led a heart.

East won the ace and returned a heart. Again, wanting to start trumps from the board, declarer crossed to dummy with a club to lead a trump. East ducked, South winning the king.

Declarer crossed again in clubs and led another spade. This time East won the ace and underled in diamonds to West. The club return and ruff meant down one.

How could declarer have prevented this?

In the other room, declarer led a diamond before playing the second club. This scissors cut the link between the defenders, preventing the later ruff.

Making four spades.

DEAL 4. SCISSORS COUP FOR DELAYED DISRUPTION

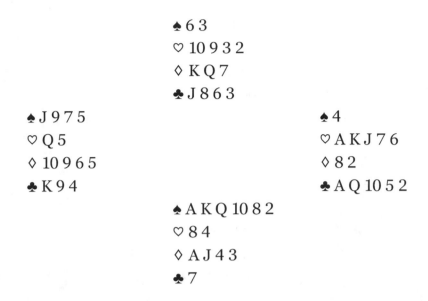

♠ 6 3
♡ 10 9 3 2
◊ K Q 7
♣ J 8 6 3

♠ J 9 7 5
♡ Q 5
◊ 10 9 6 5
♣ K 9 4

♠ 4
♡ A K J 7 6
◊ 8 2
♣ A Q 10 5 2

♠ A K Q 10 8 2
♡ 8 4
◊ A J 4 3
♣ 7

East opened 1♡ and South overcalled 1♠. Then East kept bidding his clubs and South his spades till his 3♠ bid ended the auction. West led the ♡Q, then the five to East's king. East continued with the heart ace.

South ruffed with the spade ten and West overruffed with the jack. West led a club to East who played a fourth heart. West still had ♠973 and was going to get one more trump trick regardless of how South played.

Down one, losing two hearts, one club, and two trump tricks.

How did declarer make the same contract in the other room?

Instead of getting into this trump fight, declarer discarded a club at Trick 3, a trick he was going to lose anyhow. East played a fourth round of hearts and West overruffed declarer's ten with the jack. But now West could not reach East for a further trump promotion.

Declarer made three spades, losing three hearts and one trump trick.

DEAL 5. JUST TRADING LOSERS

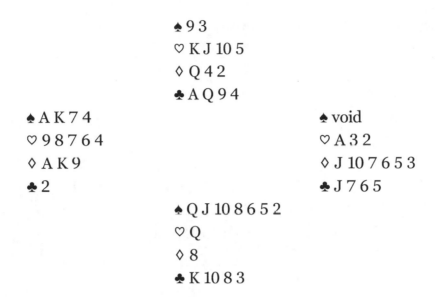

```
                      ♠ 9 3
                      ♡ K J 10 5
                      ◇ Q 4 2
                      ♣ A Q 9 4
     ♠ A K 7 4                         ♠ void
     ♡ 9 8 7 6 4                       ♡ A 3 2
     ◇ A K 9                           ◇ J 10 7 6 5 3
     ♣ 2                               ♣ J 7 6 5
                      ♠ Q J 10 8 6 5 2
                      ♡ Q
                      ◇ 8
                      ♣ K 10 8 3
```

With neither side vulnerable, South opened 3♠. Everyone passed and 3♠ became the final contract.

West led the ◇A and switched to his singleton club. Even the caddy knew this was a singleton. Declarer won and started the trumps. West won the spade king and led a heart to East's ace. The club ruff meant down one, losing three spade tricks and two aces.

"Partner, haven't you learned anything yet?" moaned North, writing minus 50 in his scorecard.

Do you think you see the solution by now?

In the other room the auction and first two tricks were the same. But this declarer, to prevent the ruff, after winning the club ace, led the diamond queen and discarded his queen of hearts. A queen for a queen.

Back on lead with the first trump trick, West could not reach East. By swapping a heart loser, declarer had cut the link. He lost two trump tricks and two diamonds.

"Well done, partner," said North, "Score it up!"

DEAL 6. WHAT'S THE HURRY?

```
                      ♠ K J 3
                      ♡ Q 7 2
                      ♦ Q J 8 5
                      ♣ A K 4
    ♠ A Q 10 9 6 4                    ♠ 8 7 5 2
    ♡ A 4                             ♡ 8
    ♦ 9 6 3 2                         ♦ A 10 7 4
    ♣ 3                               ♣ 10 8 5 2
                      ♠ void
                      ♡ K J 10 9 6 5 3
                      ♦ K
                      ♣ Q J 9 7 6
```

Non vul versus vul, West opened 2♠, a Weak Two Bid. North bid 2NT and East bid 4♠. South bid 5♡, ending the auction.

West led the ♣3, which came with a singleton label. In a hurry to draw trumps and hoping for a favorable lie of the cards, like West having only one trump, declarer led a top heart. West won and played a diamond to East. The club ruff meant down one. A little unlucky, West having two trumps, East the entry.

But the other declarer made five hearts with the same opening lead. How?

Since everyone in the room knew that the club was a singleton, South was in less of a hurry to draw trumps. Do you see how he could survive? Who, he thought, most likely had the ace of spades?

He won the opening lead in dummy and led the spade king, discarding his singleton diamond king. A king for a king seemed fair. That was the end of West reaching East.

This declarer lost one spade, the king, and the trump ace. Making five hearts.

DEAL 7. KEEPING AN OPPONENT
FROM CASHING A WINNER

```
                    ♠ A 10 5
                    ♡ Q 6 2
                    ◇ K Q 8
                    ♣ 10 7 5 4
  ♠ 6 2                              ♠ Q J 9 7 3
  ♡ A 5                              ♡ 4
  ◇ A J 10 7 3                       ◇ 9 5 2
  ♣ A Q 9 3                          ♣ K J 6 2
                    ♠ K 8 4
                    ♡ K J 10 9 8 7 3
                    ◇ 6 4
                    ♣ 8
```

West opened 1◇ and East responded 1♠. South ventured a Weak Jump Overcall, 3♡, and North gambled on 4♡.

West led the ♣6; ten, jack, king. Declarer led a diamond to dummy's king and a trump to his king.

West won the ace and led another spade. Declarer won the ace and played a trump to his hand. He led a second diamond. West took his ace and counted declarer's tricks.

If he cashed his club ace, declarer likely had ten tricks. In desperation, West led a low club. East won and cashed the spade queen.

Down one.

How did declarer in the other room take ten tricks? Poor defense?

Not at all. The other declarer, after winning the first diamond, led a low club. With this Scissors Coup, East could never get in later to cash the spade queen. West scored only his three aces.

Making four hearts.

DEAL 8. SORRY, NO TRUMP PROMOTION FOR YOU

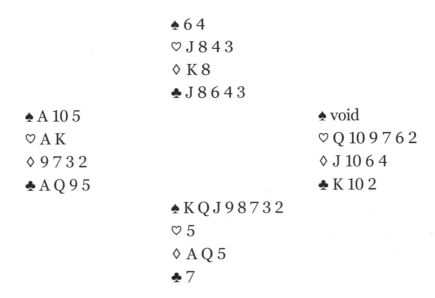

```
                        ♠ 6 4
                        ♡ J 8 4 3
                        ◊ K 8
                        ♣ J 8 6 4 3
        ♠ A 10 5                            ♠ void
        ♡ A K                               ♡ Q 10 9 7 6 2
        ◊ 9 7 3 2                           ◊ J 10 6 4
        ♣ A Q 9 5                           ♣ K 10 2
                        ♠ K Q J 9 8 7 3 2
                        ♡ 5
                        ◊ A Q 5
                        ♣ 7
```

West opened 1NT, 16 – 18 HCP. Playing Texas Transfers, East bid 4◊ to show long hearts.

South brushed it all aside bidding 4♠. West led the ♡K, then the ♡A and declarer ruffed, East playing the deuce, *surely* suit preference for clubs, as East knew the entire heart layout.

Declarer led the ♠J, but West won the ace and led the ♣9. East won the king and returned a heart, promoting West's spade ten to the setting trick.

"Nice defense," said South. North had to be restrained by his kibitzers.

What do you think North wanted to say? South made four spades in the other room.

Same old, same old. Instead of ruffing the second heart at Trick 2, the declarer in the other room just made a trade. Instead of ruffing, he discarded his club loser. No more trump promotion.

Making four spades, losing two hearts and only one spade.

DEAL 9. A QUEEN FOR A QUEEN

```
                      ♠ Q 7 6
                      ♡ A Q 4
                      ◊ 9 7 3 2
                      ♣ J 8 2
        ♠ 5 4 3                        ♠ A
        ♡ 10 9 7 6 5                   ♡ J 8 3 2
        ◊ 10 6                         ◊ A J 8 4
        ♣ 10 7 4                       ♣ A 9 6 3
                      ♠ K J 10 9 8 2
                      ♡ K
                      ◊ K Q 5
                      ♣ K Q 5
```

East opened 1◊ and South overcalled 1♠. North bid 2♠ and South bid 4♠. West led the ◊10. East played the ace (right or wrong) and returned the ◊4. Declarer won the diamond king.

When he started the trumps, East won and returned a diamond. When West ruffed, declarer finished down one.

Could this have been avoided?

East might have held up his ace one round, but declarer had missed the boat. In the other room, declarer saw that West was going to get a ruff now or later. To prevent that, when East won the ace at Trick 1 and returned a diamond, declarer won the king.

But before touching the trumps, he led the heart king to dummy's ace. Then he played the heart queen, discarding the diamond queen. A queen for a queen.

No ruff for you, Mr. West. Making four spades.

DEAL 10. CUTTING OFF THE BIG BEAR

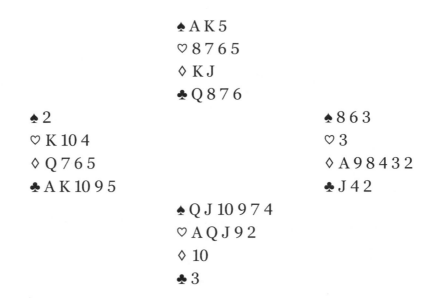

      ♠ A K 5
      ♡ 8 7 6 5
      ♢ K J
      ♣ Q 8 7 6

♠ 2   ♠ 8 6 3
♡ K 10 4   ♡ 3
♢ Q 7 6 5   ♢ A 9 8 4 3 2
♣ A K 10 9 5   ♣ J 4 2

      ♠ Q J 10 9 7 4
      ♡ A Q J 9 2
      ♢ 10
      ♣ 3

South opened 1♠ and West made a take-out double. When North redoubled, East bid 3♢, preemptive. When South bid 3♡, North bid 4♡. West led the ♣A and shifted to the ♠2.

Declarer won dummy's ace and attempted to draw trumps as quickly as possible, playing the ace, then queen. But West won as expected and led a diamond. East won the ace and gave West a spade ruff. Down one.

How did the declarer make four hearts in the other room?

The other declarer saw the handwriting on the wall. To prevent the spade ruff, after winning the spade ace, he led the club queen and discarded his diamond ten, beautifully executing a scissors coup.

You could almost hear the bear growl. Bear? Yes, this was from an old tournament. Sitting West was the bear. Bear Bryant? Tommy Prothro? I don't remember, some big guy. Making four hearts.

CHAPTER TWO

TRUMP SUIT PROBLEMS

L-O-L

TRUMP MANAGEMENT

The opportunity for Loser-On-Loser plays often arise when declaring a suit contract especially in a 4-3 trump fit. The usual trump fit consists of at least a combined holding of eight or more trumps between the dummy and declarer's hands. However, lesser holdings are sometimes necessary, and may be the only makeable contract.

A Moysian Fit refers to a declarer's 4-3 major suit trump holding, named after Alphonse (Sonny) Moyse, Jr. At times, although difficult to play, a pair, by choice, will intentionally opt to play in a major suit contract with a 4-3 trump fit as the final contract of choice.

These usually arise when either 3NT appears unsound because one suit is poorly or unstopped, or a minor suit game may be too high. These so-called Moysian trump fits are often difficult since one opponent often has as many or more pieces of trump than the declarer. Maintaining control and timing are crucial.

Declarer's dilemma is how many rounds of trump to play. Playing more than one round usually commits declarer to a given line of play, hoping the trump splits relatively evenly between the two opponents. With many Moysian fits, establishing a side suit first is often wise, or cross-ruffing in the face of the likelihood of losing trump control.

With only a slight superiority in trumps, declarer must time the play carefully on order to keep things under control. There are two primary strategies.

1) When in a game or slam contract, a controlled playing strategy is best. The necessary losing tricks are easily identified. Control is based on the timing of the trump removal, usually using the ace of trump as a control.
2) In a part score, a scramble trick-taking strategy is usually best where one's winners are identified. The basic strategy is to pitch declarer's losers on dummy's winners and by cross-ruffing.

*** Pitching losers (loser-on-loser) from the long trump hand until the short trump hand can ruff is a common strategy in the latter.

At times, a strong 4-3 fit may offer the only chance for game. For example:

North	South	
♠K54	♠AQ106	There are only 8 tricks in 3NT against good defense.
♡AJ983	♡K5	In a spade contract: four top tricks in the other suits,
♢A942	♢J875	two club ruffs in the short hand, and a likely four trump tricks
♣8	♣A93	remaining so long as West can't overruff South's ♠10 on
		the fourth round of hearts. Ten tricks.

13

DEAL 11. A PESKY 4-3

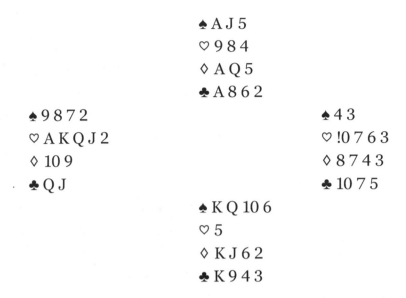

♠ A J 5
♡ 9 8 4
◊ A Q 5
♣ A 8 6 2

♠ 9 8 7 2
♡ A K Q J 2
◊ 10 9
♣ Q J

♠ 4 3
♡ !0 7 6 3
◊ 8 7 4 3
♣ 10 7 5

♠ K Q 10 6
♡ 5
◊ K J 6 2
♣ K 9 4 3

West opened 1♡ and North and East passed. South balanced with a takeout double, North cue-bid 2♡, and North-South reached 4♠.

West led the ace, then king of hearts and South ruffed.

Declarer counted ten winners. Ever the optimist, he cashed the top trumps, hoping for a 3-3 split. Sometimes suits split 3-3, but they split 4-2 more often.

Leaving West with the last trump, declarer set about cashing his tricks. He cashed the A-K of clubs, then started the diamonds. West ruffed the third diamond and cashed all his hearts.

Down two.

How would a declarer more aware of the odds play?

Yes, ten winners but in the right order. At Trick 2, to maintain control declarer discarded a club from his hand instead of ruffing. And when West persisted in hearts, declarer threw another club loser from his hand.

Now he did have ten tricks. He ruffed the next heart in dummy, drew all the trumps and claimed, losing only three hearts.

DEAL 12. OH NO, NOT AGAIN

<pre>
                        ♠ 8 7 3
                        ♡ 10 4 3
                        ◇ Q 10 9 5
                        ♣ 10 5 3
        ♠ A Q J 10 2   ♠ K 9 5 4
        ♡ 9 7   ♡ 8 6 5 2
        ◇ 6 4 3   ◇ 7
        ♣ K J 2   ♣ Q 9 8 6
                        ♠ 6
                        ♡ A K Q J
                        ◇ A K J 8 2
                        ♣ A 7 4
</pre>

After South opened 1◇, West overcalled 1♠. East bid 3♠ preemptively and South gambled 4♡. North passed, hoping 10 tricks in hearts would be easier than 11 in diamonds.

West led the ♠A and continued with another spade. Declarer again counted ten tricks and still being optimistic, ruffed the second spade. You could almost hear North screaming "No!"

Declarer tried the trumps and discovered the 4-2 split. Leaving the last trump out, he cashed the club ace, then started the diamonds. West ruffed the second diamond and cashed three spade tricks and three club tricks. Down four.

"Partner, at least save the club ace so you will only go down two again," suggested North. "Didn't you learn anything from the previous hand,' he asked?

How did a more cautious declarer play in the other room?

Same old, same old. At Trick 2, declarer discarded a club loser from his hand rather than ruff in the long trump hand. And at Trick 3? Another LOL play. And at Trick 4? Yes, draw the trumps and claim.

DEAL 13. ONE MORE FOR THE ROAD

```
                    ♠ K 10 4
                    ♡ 9 7 3
                    ♦ Q J 8 6 3
                    ♣ J 7
   ♠ 7 6 5 2                          ♠ 9 8
   ♡ A K Q 10 6                       ♡ J 8 5
   ♦ 7                                ♦ 10 9 2
   ♣ Q 8 5                            ♣ K 10 9 6 3
                    ♠ A Q J 3
                    ♡ 4 2
                    ♦ A K 5 4
                    ♣ A 4 2
```

South opened 1♦ and West bid 1♡. North bid 2♦ and South bid 2♠. North bid 3♦ over 2♠ and South cue-bid 3♡ to force once more. North bid 3♠ and South gambled 4♠.

West led the top three hearts. Declarer ruffed the third heart and optimistically tried drawing trumps.

Same old problem. When spades divided 4-2, he tried running the diamonds. West ruffed the second diamond and cashed his remaining hearts.

By now I'm sure you see the right line of play, no?

In the other room, North-South also reached 4♠. At Trick 3, this declarer discarded a club rather than ruffing. From that point, all roads led to making four spades.

DEAL 14. PLENTY OF TRUMPS BUT USE THEM WISELY

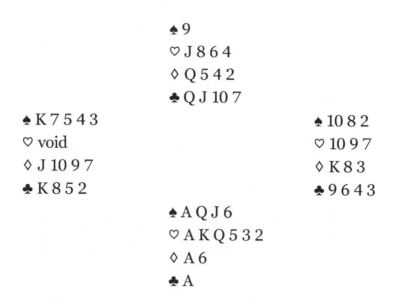

```
                    ♠ 9
                    ♡ J 8 6 4
                    ◊ Q 5 4 2
                    ♣ Q J 10 7
    ♠ K 7 5 4 3                       ♠ 10 8 2
    ♡ void                            ♡ 10 9 7
    ◊ J 10 9 7                        ◊ K 8 3
    ♣ K 8 5 2                         ♣ 9 6 4 3
                    ♠ A Q J 6
                    ♡ A K Q 5 3 2
                    ◊ A 6
                    ♣ A
```

South opened 2♣ and rebid 2♡. North bid 3♡ showing trump support and a control somewhere. South tried for six via 4◊ and 5♣ cue bids. North accepted having a singleton in the uncue-bid suit.

West led the ◊J. Trick 1 went queen, king, ace. Declarer saw no problem, ruff three spades in dummy while drawing trumps. He cashed the spade ace and ruffed a spade. A trump back to hand and another spade ruff. Whoops, East overruffed and cashed a diamond. Down one.

Unlucky or was there a better line of play?

Sure, unlucky Louie, but in the other room declarer saw a sure line of play. After winning the opening lead, she cashed the ♡AK, then the ♣A. A small trump to dummy's jack drew the last trump. Declarer led the ♣Q.

The defense was finished. If East had the ♣K and covered, declarer would ruff and have two club winners in dummy. If East played low, declarer made a LOL play, discarding her diamond loser.

If West won, declarer could win any return and ruff a spade. She would have two good clubs in dummy to discard her remaining spades. Making six hearts.

DEAL 15. THE ROAD TO ROME DESPITE A 4-1 SPLIT

```
                        ♠ Q 7 4
                        ♡ 9 6
                        ◇ Q 10 8 5
                        ♣ K 7 4 2
        ♠ 3                             ♠ 10 9 8 5
        ♡ Q J 10 8 4 3                 ♡ A K 5 2
        ◇ A 9 7 4                       ◇ 6 3
        ♣ Q J                           ♣ 10 6 3
                        ♠ A K J 6 2
                        ♡ 7
                        ◇ K J 2
                        ♣ A 9 8 5
```

South opened 1♠ and West overcalled 2♥. When the bidding war ended, South was declarer in 4♠. West led the ♥Q which held and continued another heart. Game looked easy; declarer counted five spade tricks, two club tricks, and three diamonds.

He ruffed the second heart and started the trumps. When West showed out on the second round, those ten didn't look so certain. If he drew the trumps, the defense would obtain the lead and cash hearts. If he left the trumps outstanding, he would suffer a diamond ruff and still had a club loser.

All roads led not to Rome, but to down one. "Partner," asked North, "What happened to your ten tricks?"

Did the other declarer get to Rome and take ten tricks?

Yes, the other declarer is in Rome enjoying a good dinner. Instead of ruffing at Trick 2, he made a LOL play despite have a basket full of trumps. He discarded a club from his hand at Trick 2.

If another heart was led, he could ruff in dummy and keep control. His other club loser in hand went on the long diamond.

Ten tricks, losing two hearts and one diamond. Grazie.

DEAL 16. ANOTHER 4-1 PROBLEM

```
                    ♠ K 3
                    ♡ 10 6 2
                    ◇ Q J 9 5
                    ♣ 8 5 4 2
♠ Q J 9 8 6                              ♠ A 10 7 5 2
♡ 4                                      ♡ 9 8 7 5
◇ A 7 3                                  ◇ 6 2
♣ J 9 7 3                                ♣ Q 10
                    ♠ 4
                    ♡ A K Q J 3
                    ◇ K 10 8 4
                    ♣ A K 6
```

North-South reached 4♡ after South opened 1♡. West led the ♠Q. Declarer covered with dummy's king and East won the ace. When a spade was returned, declarer faced his first problem. Ruff? Well, he had five trumps this time, so he felt comfortable ruffing.

Declarer now started drawing trumps. Of course, 4-1. If he drew all the trumps, he would have to give up the lead to the diamond ace.

So declarer stopped trumps after two rounds and started diamonds. West won the second diamond and gave East a diamond ruff. Down one.

Is 4♡ always going down?

In the other room, declarer applied the same principle we have seen in the 4-3 fits. Instead of ruffing at Trick 2, he discarded a club from his hand, a trick he would lose later anyhow. Now he maintained control.

Making four hearts, losing two spades and one diamond.

DEAL 17. TRUMP MANAGEMENT

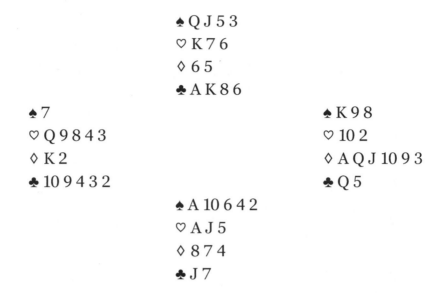

                  ♠ Q J 5 3
                  ♡ K 7 6
                  ♢ 6 5
                  ♣ A K 8 6

♠ 7   ♠ K 9 8
♡ Q 9 8 4 3   ♡ 10 2
♢ K 2   ♢ A Q J 10 9 3
♣ 10 9 4 3 2   ♣ Q 5

                  ♠ A 10 6 4 2
                  ♡ A J 5
                  ♢ 8 7 4
                  ♣ J 7

North-South reached 4♠ after East overcalled in diamonds. West led the ♢K, then the ♢2 and East continued with the ♢Q. West ruffed with the seven of trumps and declarer overruffed with the jack.

Suddenly East had a trump trick and declarer still had to lose a heart at the end. Down one.

Could you have managed your assets better?

In the other room, declarer wasn't going to get into a trump fight. When West ruffed the third diamond, she discarded a heart loser from dummy, an inevitable loser. So now West had trumped a loser, not a winner.

Declarer could now manage the trump suit for no losers. Making four spades.

DEAL 18. BEEN THERE, DONE THAT

```
                    ♠ Q 8
                    ♡ Q 10 7 5
                    ◊ A 10 7 4
                    ♣ A 7 3
♠ A K J 10 9 5                       ♠ 3 2
♡ 6                                 ♡ J 9 8
◊ J 2                               ◊ Q 9 8 5 3
♣ Q J 6 5                           ♣ 9 8 2
                    ♠ 7 6 4
                    ♡ A K 4 3 2
                    ◊ K 6
                    ♣ K 10 4
```

South opened 1♡ and West overcalled 1♠. North bid 2♠, a limit raise or better with hearts and North-South reached 4♡.

West led the ♠AK, East following and then the ♠Q. Declarer ruffed high in an attempt to win the trick.

Ruffed with what you ask? The ♡10 or Q? Does it matter? If the queen, declarer had a natural trump loser. If the ten, East overruffed. With a slow club loser yet to come, declarer was down one.

Which did the declarer in the other room choose to ruff with?

Right! Neither. The other declarer discarded a club from dummy, a trick he was due to lose anyhow, a LOL play. Then he drew trumps and claimed.

Based on a theme suggested by Alfred Sheinwold in his book "Puzzle Book #1."

DEAL 19. AVOIDING THE OVERRUFF

```
                            ♠ 9 7
                            ♡ 9 5 2
                            ◊ K 8 3
                            ♣ A J 8 5 4
        ♠ A K Q J 5 4                          ♠ 8 2
        ♡ 8 6                                  ♡ 10 4
        ◊ 10 7 2                               ◊ Q J 6 5
        ♣ 9 7                                  ♣ K Q 10 3 2
                            ♠ 10 6 3
                            ♡ A K Q J 7 3
                            ◊ A 9 4
                            ♣ 6
```

After West opened 2♠, North-South reached 4♡. West led the ♠AKQ. Declarer hopefully ruffed the third round with the ♡9, but. East overruffed with the ♡10.

With a late diamond loser still to come, the contract was down one.

A little unlucky, sort of on a heart finesse, but could you do better?

The declarer in the other room wanted to avoid these trump fights. She simply discarded a diamond from dummy at Trick 3, a card she was destined to lose.

But now she was able to ruff a diamond in the dummy.

Making four hearts. What finesse?

DEAL 20. PLEASE DON'T MAKE ME HAVE TO GUESS

```
                    ♠ Q J 9
                    ♡ A J 4 2
                    ◊ J 4 3
                    ♣ J 8 2
   ♠ 10 5 3                        ♠ A
   ♡ 9 7 5 3                       ♡ K Q 8
   ◊ 10 2                          ◊ K Q 9 8 7 5
   ♣ A K 7 4                       ♣ 9 6 3
                    ♠ K 8 7 6 4 2
                    ♡ 10 6
                    ◊ A 6
                    ♣ Q 10 5
```

East opened 1◊ and South overcalled 1♠. West's Negative Double, a common convention which showed hearts and some values, but after North raised to 2♠, everyone passed.

West led the ♣A and switched to the ◊10. South won the ace and started the trumps, leading the two to the queen. East won the ace and played the K-Q of diamonds, West following low to the second diamond.

Declarer was at the crossroads. If he ruffed low, West might overruff with the ten, down one. If he ruffed with the king, he would have to guess the spade ten.

How did the declarer who played the contract in the other room avoid this problem.?

No problem. He didn't ruff high or low. He merely discarded a heart, a trick he was going to lose later anyhow.

Making two spades, losing one spade, two diamonds, and two clubs.

DEAL 21. MAINTAINING CONTROL

♠ A K J
♡ K J
♢ A Q J 3
♣ 8 7 4 3

♠ 7 6 5 2
♡ 10 9 7 5 4
♢ 7 6
♣ Q 10

♠ 3
♡ A Q 6 3 2
♢ K 5 4
♣ J 9 6 5

♠ Q 10 9 8 4
♡ 8
♢ 10 9 8 2
♣ A K 2

North opened 1♢ and East overcalled 1♡. With a Negative Double available to show four, South's 1♠ bid showed at least five spades. West's 3♡ bid showed lots of hearts, but not a lot of HCP. North bid 3♠ and South bid game.

West led the ♡10. East won Trick 1 with the queen and continued with the heart ace. Declarer ruffed and cashed the A-K of trumps. When East showed out on the second round, declarer was in trouble.

If he drew the two outstanding trumps, East was going to regain the lead in one of the minors and would cash the rest of his hearts. If he didn't draw the trumps, his winners would be ruffed. Down one.

Was there a way to overcome the 4-1 trump split?

In the other room, the declarer was worried trumps might break badly and East was a favorite to have the diamond king. At Trick 2, instead of ruffing, he discarded the club deuce from his hand, a trick he was going to lose later anyhow.

If East persisted in hearts, he could ruff in the dummy. Now with five trumps still in hand, maintaining control was not a problem.

Making four spades, losing two hearts and one diamond.

DEAL 22. AVOIDING A PROMOTION

```
                        ♠ A 4 2
                        ♡ 10 7 2
                        ◇ Q 10 8 5 3
                        ♣ K 10
    ♠ J 9 8                              ♠ 3
    ♡ Q 8                                ♡ A K J 9 4 3
    ◇ 9 6 2                              ◇ K J 4
    ♣ 9 7 6 5 3                          ♣ 8 4 2
                        ♠ K Q 10 7 6 5
                        ♡ 6 5
                        ◇ A 7
                        ♣ A Q J
```

South opened 1♠ and North raised to 2♠. East's 3♡ overcall did not stop South from bidding 4♠.

West led the ♡Q which held, then another heart. East played a third heart. Declarer ruffed with the trump king. When he then drew trumps, West won a trump trick with the ♠ J98.

Declarer still had a diamond loser.

Down one.

"If I ruff low, he would have just overruffed," said South. North was just not interested, sadly circled minus 50, noting LOL for later.

What do you think the other North was writing?

Yes, in the other room, the declarer discarded the diamond loser on the third heart. He was in no mood to get into a trump fight. He lost only three hearts.

Making four spades, plus 420.

DEAL 23. AND FROM THE OTHER SIDE

```
                    ♠ Q 2
                    ♡ Q 10 4 2
                    ◇ A 10 7 6
                    ♣ A 7 3
♠ A K J 10 7 6                        ♠ 8 3
♡ 6                                   ♡ J 9 8
◇ 5 2                                 ◇ Q J 9 8 3
♣ Q J 9 8                             ♣ 6 5 2
                    ♠ 9 5 4
                    ♡ A K 7 5 3
                    ◇ K 4
                    ♣ K 10 4
```

South opened 1♡ and West overcalled 1♠. North bid 2♠, showing a good hand with hearts.

East passed and North-South reached 4♡.

West led the ♠AK, everyone followed, and then the ♠J. Declarer ruffed with the heart ten and East overruffed.

The late club loser meant down one, losing two spades, one club, and one trump.

"Wow!" said North. "You played this board just as well as you did at the start of the match half an hour ago when you managed somehow to turn ten tricks into nine. Are you really Rumpelstiltskin and can you also turn gold into straw?"

Should declarer have ruffed with the trump queen or what?

How about not ruffing at all, but discarding the club loser instead. This is like the previous deal, but as seen from the other side.

The other declarer made four hearts by losing three spade tricks but no club or trump tricks.

CHAPTER THREE
RUFFING PROBLEMS

DEAL 24. THE THEORY OF EMPTY SPACES

```
                    ♠ A 9 5 3
                    ♡ 10 9 8
                    ◊ A J 10 2
                    ♣ Q 3
    ♠ 8 2                              ♠ J 7
    ♡ 6 2                              ♡ A K Q 5 4 3
    ◊ 8 7 6                            ◊ 9 5
    ♣ K J 10 9 8 4   Denny             ♣ 7 6 2
                    ♠ K Q 10 6 4
                    ♡ J 7
                    ◊ K Q 4 3          Bambi
                    ♣ A 5
```

East's vulnerable Weak 2♡ bid did not keep South from overcalling 2♠, nor North from raising to 4♠. But it did keep West from leading the ♣J, which would have let South make an easy overtrick.

East won the first two tricks with high hearts and led a third high heart.

South, Denny Decimal, who taught math at a nearby college, demonstrated his knowledge for the benefit of Bambi, his admiring kibitzer.

"Theory of Empty Spaces! East has seven non-hearts, West has eleven. Odds are eleven to seven that West has the jack of spades. Therefore ..."

Denny ruffed with the ♠K, cashed the ♠Q and finessed West for the ♠J. East won, exited in clubs, and West's ♣K took the setting trick.

Could a better mathematician have avoided defeat?

The South in the other room may not have been a mathematician, but he was a better bridge player. He discarded the ♣5, a LOL on the third heart and didn't need to guess the ♠J to take the rest.

Making 4♠.

DEAL 25. TRICKERY OR QUACKERY?

$$\spadesuit\ A\ Q\ 8$$
$$\heartsuit\ Q\ J\ 10\ 9$$
$$\diamondsuit\ 8\ 7\ 6$$
$$\clubsuit\ A\ J\ 5$$

<table>
<tr><td>♠ 6 5 2</td><td></td><td>♠ 3</td></tr>
<tr><td>♡ A K 5 2</td><td></td><td>♡ 8 7 6 4</td></tr>
<tr><td>◇ Q 10 9</td><td></td><td>◇ K J 4 3</td></tr>
<tr><td>♣ 10 9 8</td><td>Pete</td><td>♣ K Q 7 2</td></tr>
</table>

$$\spadesuit\ K\ J\ 10\ 9\ 7\ 4$$
$$\heartsuit\ 3$$
$$\diamondsuit\ A\ 5\ 2$$
$$\clubsuit\ 6\ 4\ 3$$

South opened a Weak 2♠ Bid and reached 4♠. West led the ♡A, suggesting the ♡K, and switched to the ♣10 when East played low.

South, Paranoid Pete, looked at West suspiciously. "Are you trying to trick me? Would you lead the ten holding the king and queen? I think you might just be nasty enough to do so."

So he finessed dummy's ♣J. East won the ♣Q and switched to diamonds. South won the ◇A and drew trumps in three rounds but lost another club and two diamonds. 4♠ went down two.

Could declarer have done better?

Yes. In the other room, South was less concerned about trickery than tricks. He counted 10: six spades, two minor-suit aces, and two hearts. He knew he needed to set them up before he lost tricks in the minors.

Accordingly, he won dummy's ♣A at Trick 2 and threw a club on dummy's ♡10, a LOL. West won and continued clubs, but South ruffed the third club high, drew three rounds of trumps ending in dummy, and threw both his low diamonds on dummy's heart quacks. Making 4♠

DEAL 26. THE GOOD SACRIFICE

```
                    ♠ 8 5 3
                    ♡ A 2
                    ◇ Q 7 5 3
                    ♣ A 9 7 5
♠ A J                                    ♠ 7
♡ K Q 10 7 4                             ♡ J 9 8 6 5
◇ K 8                                    ◇ A J 10 9 6
♣ 10 8 3 2                               ♣ 6 4
                    ♠ K Q 10 9 6 4 2
                    ♡ 3
                    ◇ 4 2
                    ♣ K Q J
```

After East raised West's 1♡ opening to 4♡ with his "Weak Freak," South bid 4♠: automatic, on the favorable vulnerability.

West's ♡K opening lead went to dummy's ♡A, under which East dropped the ♡J. What looked like a good save now looked like a make to South ... unless, of course, West had ♠AJ7 and thus two trump tricks. South breathed a sigh of relief when East covered dummy's ♠3 with the ♠7 at Trick 2. West captured South's ♠K with the ♠A and stared at his ♡10. Suddenly he figured out why East had played the ♡J. West led the ◇K, then the ◇8 to the ◇Q and ◇A. East led a sly ◇9 and ...

West overruffed South's ♠10 with the ♠J to take the setting trick.

"Good save, pard!" said North. "We can't touch four hearts."

Well, was it?

In the other room, it wasn't. At Trick 2, declarer led dummy's ♡2 and discarded her ◇2, chirping "Following color and rank." She turned to East and said, "Just in case you're five-five in the reds, sweetheart!"

East 's face turned five shades of red as his ♡5 won Trick 2, but South ruffed the *second* diamond with the ♠10 and *made* 4♠.

DEAL 27. WEAK TRUMPS

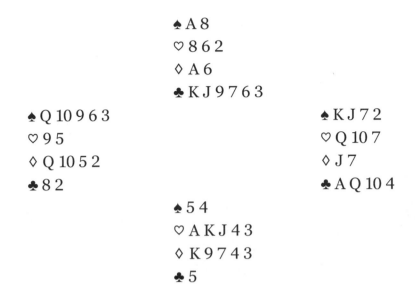

```
                        ♠ A 8
                        ♡ 8 6 2
                        ◊ A 6
                        ♣ K J 9 7 6 3
    ♠ Q 10 9 6 3                        ♠ K J 7 2
    ♡ 9 5                               ♡ Q 10 7
    ◊ Q 10 5 2                          ◊ J 7
    ♣ 8 2                               ♣ A Q 10 4
                        ♠ 5 4
                        ♡ A K J 4 3
                        ◊ K 9 7 4 3
                        ♣ 5
```

West's inability to overcall after South opened 1♡ kept his side from finding the good 4♠ save against 4♡. He led the ♠10.

South won dummy's ♠A and played on diamonds: ◊A, ◊K, diamond ruff---oops, overruff. East cashed the ♠K, exited in trump, and got a second diamond overruff. Then he tapped declarer with another spade and waited patiently to take the setting trick in clubs.

"Sorry," said North, commiserating. "I wish I'd had higher trumps for you to prevent overruffs."

Better trumps would have been nice, but were they really necessary?

Not for Paranoid Pete, who declared 4♡ in the other room. Instead of ruffing the third diamond, he discarded dummy's ♠8, a LOL. He lost that trick, an overruff of his fourth diamond, and a club at the end, but the one low trump of dummy's that didn't get overruffed supplied the tenth trick he needed to make 4♡.

DEAL 28. UNFRIENDLY HEARTS

```
                         ♠ A K 6 3
                         ♡ Q 8 4 3 2
                         ◊ J
                         ♣ K 5 2
        ♠ 5 2                                    ♠ 8 7
        ♡ K J 10 9 6                             ♡ A 7
        ◊ A K 6 3                                ◊ 10 5 4 2
        ♣ 8 7          Hannah                    ♣ Q J 10 9 3
                         ♠ Q J 10 9 4
                         ♡ 5
                         ◊ Q 9 8 7
                         ♣ A 6 4
```

North's "Flannery" 2◊ opening showing four spades, five hearts and 11 to 15 high-card points fetched an invitational 3♠ response from South. North raised to 4♠.

Using Patriarch Opening Leads, West led the ◊A and switched to the ♠2 at Trick 2. South won in hand and led the ♡5 to set up a crossruff, but West played low to let East win the ♡7 and lead his last trump.

Declarer won in dummy and crossruffed hearts and diamonds. When hearts split 5-2, he ran out of steam and tricks, scoring only five red ruffs and two top tricks in each black suit.

"Nice try," said North. "The hearts weren't very friendly," said South. Turning to West, she snarled, "You're a very mean man."

Hard-Hearted Hannah didn't inspire friendship.

In the other room Marilyn Heartthrob responded 1♠ to 1♡ and reached 4♠. The defense began similarly, but at Trick 3 South led the ◊Q and ruffed West's ◊K in dummy. East won the ♡7 next and exited in trump, but Marilyn won. She discarded dummy's ♣2 on the ◊8, a loser-on-loser play. East won the ◊10, the third and last trick for the defense. 4♠ made.

"I know which suit is *my* best friend," said Marilyn.

DEAL 29. LILYAN LULLS LAZYBONES

```
                        ♠ Q 9 4 2
                        ♡ A K 5 4
                        ◇ J 5
        Lilyan          ♣ 8 6 4          Danny
        ♠ 6                              ♠ J 8 7
        ♡ Q 10 9 3                       ♡ 8 6 2
        ◇ A K Q 9 7 4                    ◇ 10 2
        ♣ J 2           Lazybones        ♣ Q 10 9 5 3
                        ♠ A K 10 5 3
                        ♡ J 7
                        ◇ 8 6 3
                        ♣ A K 7
```

Fortunately for both of them, Lilyan and Lazybones cut on opposite teams this evening. Lazybones sleeps through mid-afternoon and Lilyan never bids diamonds. Lilyan says "Diamonds are for wearing, not bidding."

Once she won a date with Danny at her duplicate club's Christmas Party, and Danny had to invent a Notrump Defense that excluded 2◇ overcalls just to play with her. This deal occurred a week later.

Lazybones opened 1NT and reached 4♠ via "Puppet Stayman." Lilyan had no reservations about leading diamonds and led them from the top. Lazybones was wide awake enough to ruff carefully with dummy's ♠9, but Danny overruffed with the ♠J, exited with a deceptive ♣9 and won the ♣Q at the end to beat 4♠.

In the other room, Normal Norman sat West. South, Careful Kate, opened 1♠, Norman overcalled 2◇ and Kate bid 4♠ over North's invitational raise to 3♠.

Norman started with the ◇K, ◇A and ◇Q, but Kate threw the ♣4 from dummy, a loser-on-loser play, and soon claimed her contract.

DEAL 30. WASTED VALUES

```
                        Googs
                        ♠ K 9 8 2
                        ♡ void
                        ◊ A 10 5
      Mr. Smug          ♣ J 10 9 7 6 4    Willie
      ♠ 4                                 ♠ 7 3
      ♡ 10 9 8 5 2                        ♡ A Q J 7 6 4
      ◊ Q 8 7 6 3                         ◊ K J
      ♣ A 3              Mort             ♣ K Q 5
                        ♠ A Q J 10 6 5
                        ♡ K 3
                        ◊ 9 4 3
                        ♣ 8 2
```

East, Futile Willie, opened 1♡. South, Post-Mortimer Snide, overcalled 1♠, West, Mr. Smug, raised preemptively to 4♡, and North, poor Mrs. Guggenheim, took the 4♠ save on favorable vulnerability.

Mort usually waits until the post-mortem to scold his partners, but Mrs. Guggenheim is fair game from the moment she spreads her hand as dummy. West led the ♡10. As Mort ruffed in dummy, he said, "Did it ever occur to you that I might have wasted values in hearts?"

"The only thing that occurs to me is that whatever I do can turn out wrong," said the dear lady.

Mort drew trump ending in dummy and led dummy's ♣J. Willie won the ♣Q and led the ◊K, saying, "Merrimac Coup!"

Declarer ducked, won the ◊J continuation with dummy's ◊A and led another club to West's ♣A. Mr. Smug cashed the ◊Q for the setting trick.

How did 4♠ doubled fare in the other room on the ♡10 opening lead?

Very well indeed. South, the Unlucky Expert. discarded dummy's ◊5 and ◊10 on East's ♡A at Trick 1 and his own ♡K later. Ten tricks and +590.

35

DEAL 31. THE UPPERCUT

```
                    ♠ Q 10 7 5 3
                    ♡ A 7 6 5
                    ◇ A
                    ♣ K 8 3
    ♠ void                          ♠ J 9 8 6
    ♡ Q J 10 8 4                    ♡ 9 3
    ◇ K J 9 6                       ◇ 8 5 4 3
    ♣ Q 10 7 2                      ♣ J 9 4
                    ♠ A K 4 2
                    ♡ K 2
                    ◇ Q 10 7 2
                    ♣ A 6 5
```

South opened 1NT and replied 2♠ to North's Stayman 2♣. Sniffing slam, North used an artificial 3♡ rebid devised by the late Bobby Goldman of the Dallas Aces to confirm a spade fit, and then showed diamond shortness to suggest a spade slam. They used some very fancy footwork to reach 6♠.

Declarer let West's ♡Q opening lead ride to his ♡K and cashed all his side winners before crossruffing. Diamond ruff, heart---oops, East ruffed ahead of him.

"Where do you think you are, in a boxing ring? Don't you uppercut me!" he exclaimed as he overruffed with the ♠K. Another diamond ruff and another heart let East discard a diamond, In the end, West won the ♣Q and East won a trump trick: down one.

Declarer was helpless ... or was he?

In the other room, South reached 6♠ via a slightly different route and embarked on the same line of play. However, when East ruffed the third heart, South discarded his club loser and could crossruff the rest.

Yes, East would do better to discard a diamond instead of "uppercuttting," but South could still prevail.

DEAL 32. A CLAIMER

```
                    ♠ Q
                    ♡ K 10 9 5
                    ◇ K 7 5 4
                    ♣ 8 7 5 3              Mrs. Guggenheim
♠ 10 9 5 2                                 ♠ A
♡ 8 7 4 3 2                                ♡ A Q J
◇ 10 6 3                                   ◇ 9 2
♣ 6                 Willie                 ♣ K Q J 10 9 4 2
                    ♠ K J 8 7 6 4 3
                    ♡ 6
                    ◇ A Q J 8
                    ♣ A
```

East's vigorous competition in clubs pushed South to a precarious 4♠. West led the ♣6. Declarer covered with dummy's ♣7, but East recited "Third hand high!" and played the ♣K. Mrs. Guggenheim may have forgotten the ranks of the suits but she never forgot her Mother Goose.

Declarer won and led low to dummy's ♠Q. East won the ♠A and continued with the ♣Q. South suspected that West had the remaining trumps, ♠1095, and saw that ruffing high might be fatal, as that would set up two trumps for West. But he could afford to lose *one* trump trick on an overruff, so he took care to ruff with the ♠6.

When West overruffed with the ♠9 South thought he was home free, and said, "A claimer! Take your ace of hearts and I'll take the rest."

"Will you, indeed?" asked West. "I'll overruff, put Googs in with a heart, and watch you squirm, Willie, when she leads the *deuce* of clubs next." Down one, losing both major suit aces and *two* club overruffs.

Could the Unlucky Expert, South in the other room, do any better?

Yes. To deprive East of another entry, he discarded his lonely heart on the second club, a LOL play. A third club gave West her overruff, but she couldn't put East in for a trump promotion play. 4♠ made.

DEAL 33. THE RUFFING VALUE

```
                            Mrs. G
                            ♠ A 5 4 3 2
                            ♡ A 6
                            ◇ 5 4 2
                            ♣ 7 6 5
        ♠ K 10 6                              ♠ Q J 9 7
        ♡ Q J 10 5                            ♡ 3 2
        ◇ K J 9 6                             ◇ Q 10 8 3
        ♣ 4 2              Smug                ♣ 9 8 3
                            ♠ 8
                            ♡ K 9 8 7 4
                            ◇ A 7
                            ♣ A K Q J 10
```

Mr. Smug opened 1♡ and stretched a bit, jump-shifting to 3♣ and bidding 4♣ over Mrs. G's 3♠ rebid. Mrs. G duly bid 5♣.

With declarer's first suit bottled up, Futile Willie outdid himself by leading a trump to cut down on dummy's ruffing power. South won and tried to ruff out the hearts before Willie could get in to lead more trumps. East overruffed the third heart and led a diamond through. Smug won the ◇A and ruffed another heart in dummy, but East overruffed again and a second diamond lead produced the setting trick.

"Nine top tricks in three notrump," said Smug. "Why didn't you bid it?"

"Sorry. I thought I had a ruffing value," said Mrs. G.

Was she right?

In the other room, the Unlucky Expert opened 1♣ and reached 5♣ on a different auction. West, Stella by Starlight, led the ♣2. South won, took the ♡A and ♡K, and fed a heart to West, discarding dummy's ◇2.

West's ◇6 shift came too late; South won the ◇A and threw dummy's ◇5 on a fourth heart. Stella flung her cards on the table muttering "Lucky, lucky!"

5♣ makes. Dummy's diamond ruff supplies the making trick.

DEAL 34. DOUGHNUT OR DOUGHNUT HOLE?

```
                    ♠ K J 6 2
                    ♡ 10 9 5 4 2
                    ◇ A K
                    ♣ 4 2
  ♠ 9 7 5                              ♠ Q 10 4
  ♡ 7                                  ♡ J 8 6
  ◇ J 9 3                              ◇ 10 8 6 5 4
  ♣ K J 9 7 5 3      Charlie           ♣ A 6
                    ♠ A 8
                    ♡ A K Q 3
                    ◇ Q 7 2            Danny
                    ♣ Q 10 8
```

Charlie Hustle and Big Game James were friends---well, sort of---and rivals. When they cut on opposite teams, Charlie offered a side bet: "Score it also as Board-a-Match. Dime a board. At most you can lose 80 cents."

"Why not?" said James. "It's a neat addition to dollar-an-imp IMPs."

With both sides vul, Charlie opened 1NT and reached 4♡ via Stayman. West led the ♣7. Charlie took one look at dummy, then leaned over and whispered to his kibitzer. "I can almost hear another dime jingling in my pocket. Just watch: ruff a club, draw trump, spade hook, and another scrumptious glazed doughnut at Gibson's. Danny. I'll give you half."

"You're living in the past, Charlie," said Danny. "Doughnuts are a dollar at Gibson's now."

The plan went awry. East overruffed the third club. The loss of a trick to East's guarded ♠Q later meant down one. No half-doughnut for Danny.

In the other room, James was willing to settle for a doughnut hole. Same auction, same lead, but less greed. On the third club, he discarded the ♠2 from dummy, a LOL. West shifted to spades, but James won dummy's ♠K, drew trump, unblocked dummy's ◇AK, came to his hand with the ♠A and cried "Pinochle!" discarding dummy's ♠J on the ◇Q. Making 4♡. James was wrong. A pinochle is the ♠Q and ◇J. Oh, sorry, Charlie.

DEAL 35. TOUGH-LUCK TED

```
                        ♠ A 9 7 5
                        ♡ K 5 2
                        ◊ A K Q
Stella                  ♣ 5 4 3                  Danny
♠ 10 8 4                                         ♠ Q J 3
♡ 9 7 4                                          ♡ J 10
◊ J 7 6 3 2                                      ◊ 10 9
♣ 7 6                   Ted                      ♣ A K Q 9 8 2
                        ♠ K 6 2
                        ♡ A Q 8 6 3
                        ◊ 8 5 4
                        ♣ J 10
```

Danny, East, opened 1♣. South overcalled 1♡ on favorable vulnerability, Danny kept silent thereafter, eschewing a lead-directing double of North's 2♣ cue bid. Why would partner lead some other suit without a double anyway?

Soon South became declarer in 4♡. West, Stella by Starlight, led the ♣6. Danny won the ♣K, cashed the ♣A and continued with the ♣8. Ted ruffed with the ♡8.

"Got to ruff higher, Ted!" said Stella as she overruffed. She exited with the ♠4, and declarer was helpless to avoid a spade loser in the end. Down one.

"Tough luck, Ted," said Stella. "It seems Danny always has six cards for his one-club openings. Do you think I should alert them?"

"Don't," said Danny, "Thursday I opened one club with only four."

Was there no defense against a six-two club split?

Moshe was South in the other room. He found one. He discarded a spade. a LOL, on the third club and soon claimed 4♡.

DEAL 36. WILL THE REAL LOSER SIGN IN?

```
                          ♠ J
                          ♡ A K J 6 5
                          ◊ 7 4
                          ♣ A J 8 5 4
         ♠ 8 7 6 5 4                        ♠ void
         ♡ Q 10 9 7                         ♡ 8
         ◊ 8 6                              ◊ A K Q J 9 5 2
         ♣ 7 2                              ♣ K 10 9 6 3
                          ♠ A K Q 10 9 3 2
                          ♡ 4 3 2
                          ◊ 10 3
                          ♣ Q
```

In this wild and woolly deal, North opened 1♡, East bid 5◊ not knowing if it were a save or a make, and South's 5♠ ended the auction.

After losing the first two tricks in diamonds, South wondered how he would rid himself of a potential heart loser. There appeared to be three or four plausible lines ... until East led the ◊2 to Trick 3.

South discarded what he thought was his only remaining loser, the ♡2, and West followed rank with the ♣2. After ruffing with dummy's ♠J, declarer cashed dummy's ♣A and ruffed a club with the ♠2.

Curtains! West pulled the ♠4 from his hand, kissed it, and overruffed.

"Gee," he said. "I never thought this card would take the setting trick."

Did it have to? Or was West destined always to score a trick with his "five to the umpty"?

In the other room, also declaring 5♠, Henry XVIII (?!) neutralized Mr. Smug's straight flush. East, Futile Willie, played his diamonds from the top down. Henry glared at the ◊Q and said, "Oh, it's you, Anne." He flung the ♣Q on the table, saying, "And you, Catherine, you're a loser too."

He ruffed in dummy, ruffed a club low, drew trump, and dummy's ♣A provided a discard for his heart loser. Making 5♠.

DEAL 37. THE FLAW IN THE HONOR-TRICK TABLE

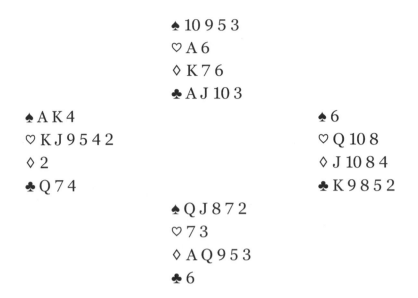

```
                    ♠ 10 9 5 3
                    ♡ A 6
                    ◊ K 7 6
                    ♣ A J 10 3
   ♠ A K 4                              ♠ 6
   ♡ K J 9 5 4 2                        ♡ Q 10 8
   ◊ 2                                  ◊ J 10 8 4
   ♣ Q 7 4                              ♣ K 9 8 5 2
                    ♠ Q J 8 7 2
                    ♡ 7 3
                    ◊ A Q 9 5 3
                    ♣ 6
```

After North opened 1♣ and South responded 1♠, West entered with 2♡. Raises of both majors prodded South to bid 4♠. West contemplated doubling, but then thought better and passed. He led the ◊2, hoping to catch East with an entry and get a ruff to beat the contract.

South captured East's ◊10 with the ◊A and tried to slip the ♠J through, but West rose with the ♠K to shift to the ♡5. Declarer won dummy's ♡A and continued trumps, but West won the ♠A, put East in with a heart, and got the diamond ruff he sought. Down one.

Did it have to be that way?

It wasn't that way in the other room, where the auction and first trick were the same. Careful Kate, South, led to dummy's ♣A and continued with the ♣J.

When East produced the ♣K, Kate ruffed. Only then did she start trumps. West won and switched to the ♡5. Kate took dummy's ♡A and shed her last heart on dummy's ♣10, a LOL. West won again, but East was bereft of entries. West tapped South with a heart, but the ♠A was the third and last trick for the defense. Making 4♠.

Culbertson's Honor Trick Table, copied by many others, shows KJ10 as 1 but does not show AJ10 as 1½. Danny claims credit for adding it.

DEAL 38. THRUST AND PARRY

                    ♠ 9 6
                    ♡ A J 9 7
                    ◊ A K Q 10 2
                    ♣ 7 2

    ♠ J 10 5   ♠ A K Q 7 4 2
    ♡ 6   ♡ K 3 2
    ◊ J 8 7 6 3   ◊ 5
    ♣ 9 8 6 4   ♣ Q J 10

                    ♠ 8 3
                    ♡ Q 10 8 5 4
                    ◊ 9 4
                    ♣ A K 5 3

North opened 1◊ in third seat. East overcalled 1♠ and as a passed hand South could respond a non-forcing 2♡. North raised to 4♡.

East overtook West's ♠J opening lead to shift to diamonds. After winning dummy's ◊10, declarer came to his hand with the ♣A to finesse in hearts. East won the ♡K, led low to West's ♠10, and scored a diamond ruff to beat 4♠. "Good shift," said South graciously.

But did South have a good counter to it?

In the other room, after the same auction and opening lead, the Unlucky Expert found the same good defense as East. But he was unlucky to be playing against Moshe. Moshe cashed both top clubs, under which East dropped the ♣J and ♣Q.

"Looks like you got me, Jack," said Moshe. "But I must give it a try."

He continued with the ♣5 and discarded dummy's last spade, a Scissors Coup. East had to overtake West's ♣8 with the ♣10. We don't call him "Unlucky" for nothing. The ♡K was the third and last trick for the defense. 4♡ made.

DEAL 39. TASTE OF HIS OWN MEDICINE

```
                        ♠ K 9 7 5
                        ♡ 4 3
                        ◇ 7 6
Arthur                  ♣ K 10 7 4 3         Barbara
♠ 10 8 4 3                                   ♠ 6 2
♡ 8 2                                        ♡ K Q J 9 7 6 5
◇ A J                                        ◇ 2
♣ A 9 6 5 2             Mort                 ♣ Q J 8
                        ♠ A Q J
                        ♡ A 10
                        ◇ K Q 10 9 8 5 4 3
                        ♣ void
```

We approve East's 4♡ opening in third seat on favorable vulnerability.

The textbooks say you need an eight-card suit but that's too rigid.

South, Post-Mortimer Snide, could no longer bid 3NT, as he might over a 3♡ opening. So he bid 5◇. West didn't have quite enough to double.

He led his doubleton ♡8. East's ♡J dislodged the ♡A. Mort tried to slip the ◇Q past West, but nothing gets by Arthur Acecasher. On a worse day, Arthur might lead the ♣A.

For the first time in his bridge career, Arthur did not try to cash the ♣A. Instead, he continued with the ♡2 to Barbara's ♡Q. Barbara's ♡5 continuation promoted a trick for Arthur's ◇J. 5◇ went down one.

"You couldn't *duck* the first heart, Mort? Taste of your own medicine!" said North. "I was helpless," said Mort. "Barbara could have had eight hearts." Well, how does Post-Mortimer Snide's medicine taste?

Phooey! Mort was right not to duck the first heart. Barbara might well have had eight. However, Mort was wrong to think he was helpless.

In the other room, the Unlucky Expert also opened 4♡ and Moshe declared 5◇. But at Trick 2, Moshe crossed to dummy's ♠K and dumped the ♡10 on dummy's ♣K, a Scissors Coup cutting the link between defenders' hands.

Making 5◇.

DEAL 40. LARYNGITIS!

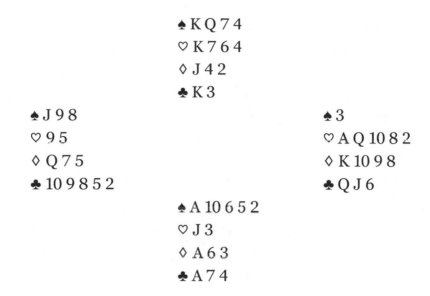

♠ K Q 7 4
♡ K 7 6 4
◇ J 4 2
♣ K 3

♠ J 9 8
♡ 9 5
◇ Q 7 5
♣ 10 9 8 5 2

♠ 3
♡ A Q 10 8 2
◇ K 10 9 8
♣ Q J 6

♠ A 10 6 5 2
♡ J 3
◇ A 6 3
♣ A 7 4

East opened 1♡ on favorable vulnerability, South overcalled 1♠, and North raised to 4♠ despite the ill-placement of his ♡K. After all, the ♡K might not be entirely worthless.

West led the ♡9. East won the first two tricks in hearts and continued the ♡10. Play stopped while South performed "Eeny, meany, miney, moe" on the fingers of both hands, muttering, "Two-two split or jack on side?"

Finally, she muttered, "Guess I'll play the opening bidder for any missing honor," and ruffed with the ♠10. West overruffed. Eventually, declarer discarded one diamond on dummy's ♡K but still had a diamond loser. Down one.

"Sorry, partner," said South afterwards. "Guess I guessed wrong. 'Eeny, meany, miney, moe' doesn't seem to work for me any more.

Can you recommend something better?"

In the other room, South had laryngitis and couldn't perform the familiar children's ritual. Instead, faced with the same defense against 4♠, she tried a loser-on-loser play. She discarded one low diamond on the third heart, allowing West to ruff low.

Later, after drawing the rest of the trumps, she discarded her other low diamond on dummy's ♡K. Making 4♠.

DEAL 41. "OOH, YOU'RE A HOLIDAY"

```
              ♠ Q J 7 3
              ♡ K 8 7 6
              ◊ A 10
              ♣ 5 4 2
♠ 4 2                          ♠ A K 10 9 6
♡ J 10 4                       ♡ void
◊ Q 7 5 4 2                    ◊ K J 8 6
♣ J 10 7      Denny           ♣ Q 9 8 3
              ♠ 8 5
              ♡ A Q 9 5 3 2
              ◊ 9 3            Bambi
              ♣ A K 6
```

Favorable vulnerability induced East to risk a 3♠ overcall after North raised South's 1♡ opening to 3♡. South, Denny Decimal, didn't need to perform any mathematical calculations to bid 4♡.

West led a dutiful ♠4 to dummy's ♠J and East's ♠K. Despite Denny's falsecard of the ♠8. East continued with the ♠A and then the ♠10, suit preference for diamonds, while giving his partner a ruff.

For the benefit of Bambi, his kibitzer, Denny reasoned aloud, "The chance of a second heart being with the first is 12/25, aka Christmas. The chance of a third heart being with the first two is 11/24, just the date on which Thanksgiving falls this year. That's how you can remember it. The product of the two holidays is 22%, so ruffing high offers 78% chances. Who could ask for anything more?"

With that, Denny played the ♡A. He was able to throw a diamond on dummy's ♠Q later, but he lost a heart and a club. Down one.

Did Moshe, South in the other room, fare any better?

Yes. He threw a diamond on the third spade, a loser-on-loser, letting West ruff, and a club on dummy's ♠Q after trumps were gone. Making 4♡.

Denny's math? Not exactly right, and a turkey idea here.

DEAL 42. CAN'T TEACH 'EM AND BEAT 'EM

```
                    ♠ K Q 7 4
                    ♡ K 7 6 4
                    ◊ J 4 2
                    ♣ K 3                    Bambi
    ♠ J 10 9                                 ♠ 3
    ♡ 9 5                                     ♡ A Q 10 3 2
    ◊ Q 7 5                                   ◊ K 10 9 8
    ♣ 10 9 8 5 2        Denny                 ♣ Q J 6
                    ♠ A 8 6 5 2
                    ♡ J 8
                    ◊ A 6 3
                    ♣ A 7 4
```

One day, Bambi decided to get her feet wet. She joined the team game. Soon she found herself playing against Denny Decimal himself. North, a rigid 4-3-2-1 point-counter and strict five-card majorite, thought he had 12 HCP and opened 1◊. Bambi had ample values for her 1♡ overcall, Denny responded 1♠ and jumped to 4♠ over Smug's 2♠ raise.

West led the ♡9. "Glad I got my lead-director in," said Bambi when she saw dummy.

"Ssshhh, Honey," said Denny. "You can wait till the deal is over."

Remembering the similar deal on which Denny had failed recently, Bambi won her two heart tricks andd a third.

"Easter fell on 4/10 this year, and by sheer coincidence, that's the probability of a 2-2 split," said Denny. "That makes me an underdog, but at least it's better than 22%. He ruffed with the ♠A and cashed dummy's ♠K and ♠Q. He discarded the ◊3 on dummy's ♡K and said "Loser on loser," as West ruffed with the ♠J. Eventually he lost a diamond. "Down only one," he said, but I do no better if I ruff low."

In the other room, Moshe declared 3♠ after North passed as dealer. Moshe faced the same defense. "Didn't I see a deal like this before?" he asked as he discarded a diamond on the third heart. An overtrick and +170.

DEAL 43. CAN THERE BE TOO MUCH OF A GOOD THING?

```
                        ♠ Q 7
                        ♡ K 8 4 2
                        ◊ K 9 8 7 2
                        ♣ 9 2
        ♠ A K J 9 6 5                        ♠ 8 3
        ♡ 10                                 ♡ J 9 7
        ◊ A 10 5                             ◊ J 4 3
        ♣ K J 7          Lola                ♣ Q 10 6 5 3
                        ♠ 10 4 2
                        ♡ A Q 6 5 3
                        ◊ Q 6          Jim
                        ♣ A 8 4
```

Lola had learned from Danny to devalue her doubleton queen. She passed as dealer but balanced with 2♡ when West's 1♠ opening came round to her. West's 2♠ rebid pushed North to 3♡.

West led spades from the top. When he continued with the ♠J, Lola discarded the ♣2 from dummy. West led a fourth spade. Lola, who is anything but a LOL, threw the ◊2 from dummy. Placing a palm on her kibitzer's thigh she said, "Don't think this 'LOL' learned nothing from your LOL book with Danny!'"

East, who had already shed the ◊3 at Trick 3, shed the ◊4 at Trick 4.

After ruffing the fourth spade in hand, Lola cashed the ♣A and ruffed a club in dummy. Having one more club to ruff, she led to her ◊Q. West won the ◊A and gave East a diamond ruff. Down one!

Jim was livid. "How could you have read our book on LOL? Danny and I haven't even finished writing it."

Lola smiled and said, "Whatever Lola wants, Lola gets."

In the other room, Moshe had also been pushed to 3♡. He too threw dummy's ♣2 on the third spade. He ruffed the fourth spade in dummy. Whether East discarded again or overruffed, she was helpless. 3♡ made.

48

DEAL 44. NO FINESSE WITHOUT AN ENTRY?

                      ♠ A J 2
                      ♡ K Q 5
                      ◇ 10 8 6
                      ♣ A Q 4 3
    ♠ 9 7 6   ♠ K Q 10 5 3
    ♡ A J 10   ♡ 8
    ◇ 3   ◇ A 9 7 4 2
    ♣ K 10 8 7 6 2   ♣ J 5
                      ♠ 8 4
                      ♡ 9 7 6 4 3 2
    Danny   ◇ K Q J 5
                      ♣ 9

North opened 1NT and East overcalled 2♠. West alerted, and South asked what it meant. When West answered "Cappelletti," Southwest, Danny, objected, "Friends of Fred say 'Hamilton, spades and a minor.'"

South bid 2NT, North announced, "Lebensohl," and West passed. North bid 3♣ as the popular Lebensohl convention required. South's discouraging 3♡ rebid (weaker than a direct 3♡) ended the auction.

The defenders won the first two tricks with a diamond to the ◇A and a diamond ruff. Declarer won West's spade shift in dummy, and drove out West's ♡A with dummy's ♡K. East won West's spade continuation and gave West another diamond ruff to beat 3♡.

Could declarer have overcome the 5-1 diamond split?

In the other room, East's overcall was a "Roth-Stone ASTRO" 2◇ showing spades and diamonds specifically. Moshe, South, bid a natural 2♡ and North's 3♡ raise over West's 2♠ ended the auction. The first three tricks were the same. At Trick 4, Moshe turned to West and said, "I'm finessing you for the king of clubs."

"Bet you can't, as you're on the board," said Mae, West. "Quarter?"

Moshe cashed dummy's ♣A and threw the ♠8 on dummy's ♣Q when East followed low. Mae won the ♣K, but paid out 140 points and 25 cents.

DEAL 45. WHICH GAMBLES?

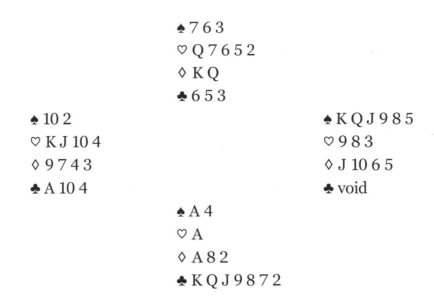

```
                        ♠ 7 6 3
                        ♡ Q 7 6 5 2
                        ◇ K Q
                        ♣ 6 5 3
      ♠ 10 2                                ♠ K Q J 9 8 5
      ♡ K J 10 4                            ♡ 9 8 3
      ◇ 9 7 4 3                             ◇ J 10 6 5
      ♣ A 10 4                              ♣ void
                        ♠ A 4
                        ♡ A
                        ◇ A 8 2
                        ♣ K Q J 9 8 7 2
```

East opened 3♠ on favorable vulnerability in third seat. Would you gamble 3NT with the South hand? This South gambled 5♣ instead, and West gambled a double.

West led the ♠10. East overtook with the ♠J. If East had only six spades, possible on this vulnerability, South could ensure his doubled contract by ducking. But betting on East's having only six spades was a bad gamble, so South won the ♠A before it could go South.

So South gambled on a likely 7-1 spade split, winning the ♠A and leading the ♣K to drive out West's ♣A. Curtains! East won West's ♣2 continuation and led the ♠K to promote a trump trick for West's ♣10. Down one.

Was a better gamble available?

In the other room, the Unlucky Expert gambled 5♣ over Futile Willie's 3♠ but he escaped the double ... and tried more of his chances.

Willie overtook Mrs. G's ♠10 lead and South didn't dare duck. But before touching trump, South cashed the ♡A, led to dummy's ◇Q and threw his ♠4 on dummy's ♡Q, a Scissors Coup. Googs won and continued the ♠2. South ruffed, drove out the ♣A and claimed.

"Glad I didn't double," said Mrs. Guggenheim. " I never double Jack."

DEAL 46. WHOM DO YOU THINK YOU'RE FOOLING?

```
                        ♠ A 10
                        ♡ Q 9 7 3
                        ◊ J 9
         Mrs. G         ♣ K Q 10 8 6      Moshe
         ♠ 8 7 5 3                         ♠ Q J 4 2
         ♡ 6 5                             ♡ A 8
         ◊ Q 4 2                           ◊ A K 10 8 5 3
         ♣ 9 7 5 2                         ♣ 3
                        ♠ K 9 6
                        ♡ K J 10 4 2
                        ◊ 7 6
                        ♣ A J 4
```

East, Moshe, opened 1◊, South overcalled 1♡ and soon reached 4♡. Mrs. Guggenheim, West, led the ◊2. Moshe won the ◊A and shifted to the ♣3. Declarer captured Mrs. G's ♣9 with dummy's ♣10 and led a low heart from dummy, but Moshe rose with the ♡A to continue diamonds.

Googs won the ◊Q and bent over to see if somebody's ◊K had fallen to the floor. Puzzled when she didn't see it, she shrugged her shoulders and led the ♣2. Moshe ruffed with the ♡8. Mr. Smug, South, claimed the rest. Down one.

Googs glared at Moshe. "You're as bad as Willie," she said. "He falsecards too. You fooled me into thinking the diamond king was missing."

As it happened, Futile Willie was East in the other room. Did he find the same killing defense as Moshe?

Not exactly. For once, Willie didn't falsecard at Trick 1 when West led the ◊2 against 4♡. South, the Unlucky Expert, put up dummy's ◊J. Willie won the ◊K and outdid himself with a killing ♣3 shift.

South won the ♣A, led to dummy's ♠A and continued with dummy's ♠10 to Willie's ♠Q and his own ♠A. When South led the ♠9 and discarded dummy's ◊9, Willie grinned and said, "Ruffing finesse, Jack? Loses!" as he won the ♠J. But that was the third and last trick for the defense. 4♡ made.

DEAL 47. ROLL WITH THE PUNCH

```
                    ♠ J 10 4 2
                    ♡ 8 7 6 3
                    ◇ K 6 4
                    ♣ K J
♠ A K Q 9 7                              ♠ 6
♡ 10 5 4                                 ♡ J
◇ J 9                                    ◇ A Q 8 5 3 2
♣ 10 6 3         Suki                    ♣ 9 7 5 4 2
                    ♠ 8 5 3
                    ♡ A K Q 9 2
                    ◇ 10 7
                    ♣ A Q 8
```

South, Suki the feminist bridge teacher, opened 1♡ in fourth seat, West overcalled 1♠, and North's 2♡ raise ended the auction.

West led the ♠K, showing the ♠Q, and continued with the ♠A, clarifying his holding. East discarded the ♣2 and followed with the ♣9 when West cashed the ♠Q. West read East's ♣9 discard as intended, suit preference for spades based on a trump high enough to uppercut.

"One black nine deserves another," said West as he led the ♠9.

East, a former welterweight champion of Waukegan, cried "Socko, whammo!" as he ruffed with the ♡J and feigned an uppercut with his fist.

"Girls are better," countered Suki as she overruffed with the ♡Q. When the ♡A and ♡K failed to fell the ♡10, Suki tried her last chance, leading to dummy's ◇K. West having passed as dealer, it was bound to lose. East won the ◇A and ◇Q; West's ♡10 took the setting trick.

"Kings are overrated. and so is the Law of Total Trumps," said Suki. "With nine in the combined hands, I'm supposed to be safe in three hearts, but I couldn't even make two."

Was she right?

We'd hate to argue with Suki, but when the Unlucky Expert declared 2♡ in the other room, he discarded the ◇7 on the fourth spade, making 2♡.

DEAL 48. CAN A LONG CARD BE A LOSER?

```
                        ♠ Q 3
                        ♡ J 3
                        ◊ A 9 4 2
    Willie              ♣ K 10 8 5 3       Smug
    ♠ A K J 8 6 5                          ♠ 7 2
    ♡ A 10 4                               ♡ 9 7 6 5 2
    ◊ Q 10 3                               ◊ J 8 6
    ♣ 7                 Mrs. G             ♣ J 9 6
                        ♠ 10 9 4
                        ♡ K Q 8
                        ◊ K 7 5
                        ♣ A Q 4 2
```

West overcalled 1♠ but was not strong enough to act again when North's 3♣ "limit raise" came round to him. He led spades from the top, continuing with the ♠J when East signaled high-low to show a doubleton.

"I wish I had a loser to discard from dummy, but I don't" said South, Mrs. Guggenheim. "Jack has been teaching me about Loser-on-Losers."

With that she thought about how high to trump, and finally selected dummy's ♣10 as a reasonable compromise.

Oops, Mr. Smug had the ♣J and overruffed. Subsequent heart and diamond losers put 3♣ down one.

"Maybe I should have ruffed with the king and led the ten next for a finesse," said Mrs. G.

"Wouldn't have helped," said Smug. "I'd have covered, and covered dummy's eight next round. Then my six of clubs would have stood up."

"And of my club seven you say nothing?" added Willie.

Well, dear reader, were any of them right?

None of this bunch was right, of course. In the other room, where the Unlucky Expert had volunteered to play with Bambi, he too declared 3♣. On the third spade, he threw the ◊2 from dummy, an early LOL. Later, he set up a heart discard for another of dummy's diamonds. He made 3♣.

DEAL 49. DANNY'S "BERRIES"

```
                        ♠ 7 3 2
                        ♡ A J 6 5 3
                        ◊ 5 2
                        ♣ A 6 4
Smug                                        Moshe
♠ 5 4                                       ♠ 8 6
♡ Q 9                                       ♡ K 10 8 7 2
◊ K Q J 8 7 4                               ◊ A 9
♣ Q 10 9                Denny               ♣ J 8 3 2
                        ♠ A K Q J 10 9
                        ♡ 4
                        ◊ 10 6 3
                        ♣ K 7 5
```

Moshe likes Weak Two-Bids, but only in the majors. However, Mr. Smug outstubborned him and they were playing Weak 2◊ Bids too. Moshe suffers from a severe case of spadophobia, so he raised Smug's 2◊ to 3◊ preemptively. This forced Denny Decimal to bid spades at the three-level, and North raised to 4♠.

Moshe overtook Smug's ◊K opening lead with the ◊A and Smug returned the favor by overtaking Moshe's ◊9 with the ◊J despite Denny's sly failure to cover. Smug's ◊Q continuation brought a smile to Denny's face as he pondered his play from dummy.

As he does in his math classes, he lectured his playmates here. "My friend Danny has a measure of suit quality he calls *berries*. He adds for spot-cards as low as the eight. Perhaps he should count sevens too. There's a 50% chance dummy's seven of trump will be worth a full trick."

With that, he played the ♠7 from dummy. "Your 50% just became zero, Denny," said Smug as Moshe overruffed. A club loser beat 4♠ one.

In the other room, East bid 2♡ over West's Weak 2◊ Bid. The Unlucky Expert raised Mrs. Guggenheim's 2♠ to 3♠. She was happy to pass. On the third diamond, seeing that her contract was secure, she said, "This is a good time to practice LOL," and threw dummy's ♣4. She made an *overtrick*.

CHAPTER FOUR

ENDPLAYS AND L - O - L

DEAL 50. A "WILLIE SAFETY PLAY"

```
                    ♠ Q 10 7
                    ♡ 10 9 8 2
                    ◊ A 9 7
                    ♣ 6 4 2              Mrs. G
 ♠ 3                                     ♠ 8 6
 ♡ A K J 7 5                             ♡ 6 4 3
 ◊ Q 10 8 5                              ◊ K J 6 3
 ♣ K 8 3             Willie              ♣ J 10 9 7
                    ♠ A K J 9 5 4 2
                    ♡ Q
                    ◊ 4 2
                    ♣ A Q 5
```

Futile Willie opened 1♠, but jumped to 4♠ when West's 2♡ overcall came round to him. West led hearts from the top, but Willie ruffed the ♡K, saying, "You don't think I'd bid four spades with *two* hearts, do you?"

He used dummy's trump honors as entries to ruff two more hearts, taking care to preserve his ♠5 in case he needed a late entry to dummy for a club finesse. Then he led to dummy's ◊A and came off dummy with another diamond, but Mrs. Guggenheim, East, rose with the ◊K and smiled.

She turned to Willie and said, "I've seen you before. Don't think you can steal a trick with a doubleton queen on me. Besides, I read Jim and Danny's book on when to play second hand high instead of low."

Then she shifted smartly to the ♣J. Willie rose with the ♣A, saying, "I can play second hand high too! Just in case your partner has a singleton king. If you have the king, I can lead through it later. A *Willie Safety Play!*"

No luck, down one. Could South make 4♠ in the other room?

There the Unlucky Expert reached 4♠ on a different auction. Instead of ruffing the second heart, he discarded the ◊2, his first LOL play. West's ◊5 shift dislodged dummy's ◊A, but after drawing trump with the ♠A and ♠Q, South threw a club on dummy's ♡10, a *second* LOL play. Dummy's ♡9 was declarer's tenth trick. 4♠ made

DEAL 51. ONE GOOD CHANCE

Smug
- ♠ 7 5
- ♡ K 4 2
- ◊ A Q 4
- ♣ A K 6 4 2

♠ 9 8 6		♠ 4 3
♡ Q J 10 8 5		♡ 9 7 6 3
◊ J 9 7		◊ K 8 3
♣ J 9	Mrs. G	♣ Q 10 7 5

Mrs. G
- ♠ A K Q J 10 2
- ♡ A
- ◊ 10 6 5 2
- ♣ 8 3

Mr. Smug, North, responded 2♣ to South's 1♠ opening. After Mrs. Guggenheim jump-rebid 3♠, he Blackwooded. Upon learning that a king was missing, he stopped in 6♠.

West led the ♡Q. As Smug spread the dummy, he said, "Be very careful. Try *all* your chances." Googs won the ♡A, drew trumps pitching the ♡2 from dummy, cashed ♣AK and ruffed a club.

When West discarded, that was one chance tried and failed. Next she finessed the ◊Q, When East won the ◊K, that was a second chance tried and failed. East returned the ◊8. She put up the ◊10, but West covered with the ◊J, and her third chance went down the drain.

The ♡K provided only one discard. She lost another diamond. Down one.

"Good try, Googs!" said Mr. Smug, his first kind words to her in months.

But did Mrs. Guggenheim miss another chance?

In the other room, the Unlucky Expert reached 6♠ by another route and the play began the same. However, when East covered dummy's third club, he discarded the ◊2, a LOL. East's heart exit gave him a second diamond discard and the entry he needed to ruff out clubs for a third.

6♠ made.

DEAL 52. A BALANCING ACT

```
                        ♠ 8 7 6 3
                        ♡ A 6
                        ◊ A 6 5 4 2
Mrs. G                  ♣ 5 2              Unlucky Expert
♠ A K 10                                   ♠ Q J 9 4
♡ Q 8                                      ♡ J 4 3
◊ K J 10                                   ◊ Q 7 3
♣ Q 10 7 4 3           Mr. Smug            ♣ J 9 8
                        ♠ 5 2
                        ♡ K 10 9 7 5 2
                        ◊ 9 8
                        ♣ A K 6
```

When neither side is vulnerable, both sides often combine for balancing acts. West dealt and opened 1NT, South balanced with 2♡. East, the Unlucky Expert, didn't relish defending with Mrs. Guggenheim and balanced with 2♠, and North (need we name him?) balanced with 3♡. You might think they were playing matchpoints, not IMPs.

West led and continued spades. South ruffed the third spade, cashed the ♡A and both top clubs and ruffed a club. Then, ◊A, diamond to West's ◊J---oops, sorry, East put up the ◊Q. When East continued with a fourth spade, South ruffed with the ♡7, but even Mrs. Guggenheim knew to overruff with the ♡Q. Declarer had to lose a trick to East's ♡J. Down one.

Was this loss necessary?

In the other room, only South, Careful Kate, balanced. She bought the contract for 2♡. The play began the same, but after ruffing a club in dummy, Kate saw a chance for a 1-IMP overtrick. She led dummy's last spade and discarded the ◊9. She lost only three spades and one heart, plus 140. Yes, a 5-IMP pickup instead of a mere 4 IMPs.

Analysts who study team matches might ask themselves, "Who deserves the credit? Who deserves the blame?" for swings like this one.

DEAL 53. BETTER GO BACK, JACK, DO IT AGAIN

```
                    ♠ A K Q 8
                    ♡ void
                    ◇ J 8 4 2
                    ♣ 10 8 7 6 2
    ♠ J 5 2                          ♠ 10 7 6 3
    ♡ J 4                            ♡ A 5 3 2
    ◇ K 10 6 5                       ◇ A Q 7
    ♣ K Q J 5      Willie            ♣ 4 3
                    ♠ 9 4
                    ♡ K Q 10 9 8 7 6
                    ◇ 9 3
                    ♣ A 9
```

Vul against not, Futile Willie was torn between a Weak 2♡ Bid and a full-fledged 3♡ preempt in third seat. He resolved his dilemma by opening 4♡. That bought the contract.

Willie won West's ♣K opening lead with the ♣A and knew to take dummy's top spades to discard a club before touching trumps. Then he ruffed a club to reach his hand and start trumps with the ♡Q. East won the ♡A, cashed the ◇A and on seeing West's encouraging ◇10, continued with the ◇Q, which held.

Then he led the ♠10. Willie ruffed with the ♡10, but West overruffed with the ♡J, the setting trick. "Just my bad luck," said Willie. "I couldn't pick up the jack of trump."

But could somebody else have done so?

In the other room, North was Mr. Smug, who counted 13 points, 10 in high cards, 3 for his void. He opened 1◇ to prepare a 2♣ rebid over a 1NT response, but rebid 1♠ over the Unlucky Expert's 1♡. He could only frown and pass the Expert's 4♡ rebid.

After winning the ♣K lead in hand, the Expert played all four of dummy's spades, discarding diamonds. East won the fourth spade, but a club and the ♡A were the only other tricks for the defenders. 4♡ made.

DEAL 54. ARE 5-TO-2 ODDS ENOUGH?

```
                        ♠ A J 8 5
                        ♡ A 8 5 3
                        ◊ K 6
        Mrs. G          ♣ 9 6 2
        ♠ 4                             ♠ 6 3
        ♡ K Q J 9 6 4 2                 ♡ 10
        ◊ J 8 7                         ◊ Q 10 5 3 2
        ♣ K 10          Denny           ♣ J 8 7 5 4
                        ♠ K Q 10 9 7 2
                        ♡ 7
                        ◊ A 9 4
                        ♣ A Q 3
```

Vul against not, Mrs. Guggenheim, West, opened 3♡. South, Denny Decimal, had far more than enough for his balancing 3♠, so he bid 6♠ directly over North's 4♡ cue bid.

Mrs. G led the ♡K to dummy's ♡A. Denny stripped the red suits while drawing trump. With only black cards left he led dummy's ♣2 and covered East's ♣7 with the ♣Q. "I'm a five-to-two favorite, maybe even six-to-one," he said.

Mrs. G won the ♣K and exited with the ♣10. "If you'd had that ten, Pard, I'd have led it and let it ride, ensuring the slam," said Denny. However, after capturing the ♣10 with his ♣A, he had no way to avoid a second club loser. Bad luck, down one.

But did South really need any luck in clubs?

No. In the other room, the Unlucky Expert reached the same ending but led dummy's last heart and discarded the ♣3, an LOL play. West won. The Expert said, "Ruff-sluff or come to me in clubs, Stella."

Stella by Starlight folded her cards, saying "Lucky, lucky!" 6♠ made.

DEAL 55. FINESSE RAPPORT

Mrs. G
♠ A Q 6 5 3 2
♡ A Q J 8
◇ J 6
♣ 4

Willie
♠ 7
♡ 7 5 2
◇ K Q 8 5 4 2
♣ 9 8 5

Mr. Smug
♠ K 10
♡ K 10 9 4
◇ 7
♣ A K Q 10 6 3

Denny
♠ J 9 8 4
♡ 6 3
◇ A 10 9 3
♣ J 7 2

Mrs. Guggenheim might have settled for a 2♠ overcall over Willie's 2◇ Weak Jump Shift, but she doubled to bring hearts into the picture. Didn't Mr. Smug tell her just last week that any contract figured to play better from her partner's side than her own?

Whether from obliviousness to the auction or from fear of a penalty pass, Smug bid 2♡. South eked out a 2♠ bid and North raised to 4♠.

Smug won the club lead and shifted to the ◇7. Denny won the ◇A and lost a spade finesse to East's ♠K. He won East's ♠10 return with the ♠J and lost a heart finesse. One loser in each suit meant down one.

"Both finesses lost, only a 25% chance," said Denny. "I guess my usual Finesse Rapport isn't working for me tonight."

Might South in the other room have had better Finesse Rapport?

There the Unlucky Expert, who also declared 4♠ as South, knew he lacked Finesse Rapport. Upon winning the ◇A at Trick 2, he did not waste his entry on a spade finesse that was likely to lose.

Instead he ruffed the ♣7 in dummy, cashed the ♠A and threw East in with the ♠K. He threw dummy's ◇J on East's ♣A. East had to offer a sluff-ruff or lead into dummy's hearts. South lost one spade and two clubs but no other tricks. 4♠ made.

DEAL 56. THE SQUEEZE

```
                    ♠ Q 4
                    ♡ 9 8 6
                    ◊ K 7 5 3
                    ♣ A 6 5 2            Stella by Starlight
    ♠ A 8 6 2                            ♠ 5 3
    ♡ A K J 10 5 3                       ♡ Q 2
    ◊ 4                                  ◊ Q J 10 8 2
    ♣ 8 3            Perfect Patti       ♣ J 10 9 7
                    ♠ K J 10 9 7
                    ♡ 7 4
                    ◊ A 9 6
                    ♣ K Q 4
```

With nobody vul, players overcompete for partscores, almost as if they were playing matchpoints. Sometimes even players who know they're playing IMPs, go overboard trying for overtricks.

But don't double lightly at IMPs. Warned that his contract is in danger, even an overtrick hog may try to lock it up.

South, Perfect Patti, overcalled 2♠ after East responded 1NT to West's 1♡ opening. West competed to 3♡ and Patti balanced with a double.

With no safer option, North retreated to 3♠. That ended the auction.

West led hearts from the top, ♡AKJ. East discarded the ◊2. Seeing only one more loser, the ♠A, Patti ruffed. She slipped the ♠9 by West and continued the ♠K. West won the ♠A and led a fourth heart. Patti ruffed and led the ♠J, her last. Stella couldn't guard both minors. When Patti announced "Squeeze for an overtrick." Stella started to throw her hand in.

West displayed the ♠8 and ♡53."I get these," he said. Down two.

Could Patti have done better?

In the other room, West doubled 3♠. Warned of a 4-2 trump split, South discarded the ◊6 on the third heart, loser on loser. She ruffed the next heart with dummy's ♠Q and lost only to the ♠A. Making 3♠ doubled.

DEAL 57. TAKING THREE CHANCES

```
                        ♠ A Q 10 9
                        ♡ A K 8 6
                        ◇ K 7
        Mrs. G          ♣ 8 6 5
        ♠ 6 4                               ♠ 5 3
        ♡ J 10 9 3                          ♡ 7 5 2
        ◇ 10 8 5 2                          ◇ J 9 6 4 3
        ♣ K J 7         Willie              ♣ 10 9 4
                        ♠ K J 8 7 2
                        ♡ Q 4
                        ◇ A Q
                        ♣ A Q 3 2
```

After South, Futile Willie, opened 1♠, a "Jacoby Forcing Raise" followed by Roman Keycard Blackwood landed him in 6♠.

Willie, set out to take "all his chances." He won West's ♡J opening lead in hand, drew trump, and took dummy's top hearts to discard the ♣2. He ruffed dummy's last heart to strip the suit and cashed the ◇A. He was about to strip diamonds when he thought: what if the club king is off?

Two more chances! Googs might have a singleton ♣K. Or if she had another, he might endplay her by cashing the ♣A *before* leading to his ♣Q. Like Archimedes emerging from his bath, he cried "Eureka!" He led ♣A, ◇Q to dummy's ◇K, low to the ♣Q …

Googs won the ♣K, led the ♣J and said, "Sorry, dear, I have this too."

"Took all three of my chances," said Willie as he marked down one on his scorecard.

But was there a better chance that might have worked?

At the other table, the Unlucky Expert reached 6♠ via a different route. He won the ♡Q, drew trump, and stripped only diamonds. Then he took dummy's ♡AK and threw the ♣2. When East discarded on dummy's ♡8, he threw the ♣3, *one* LOL, and claimed. West surrendered. 6♠ made.

DEAL 58. FOUR CHANCES?

```
                        ♠ J 7
                        ♡ Q 10 9 8
                        ◊ 7 6 5
Bear                    ♣ A J 4 3
♠ K Q 10 9 3                              ♠ 8 6 5 4 2
♡ 2                                       ♡ 3
◊ K 8 4 3 2                               ◊ J 10 9
♣ 3 2                   Denny             ♣ Q 10 9 8
                        ♠ A
                        ♡ A K J 7 6 5 4
                        ◊ A Q
                        ♣ K 7 6
```

Adverse vulnerability deterred West from intervening over South's Omnibus 2♣ opening. North "waited" with a neutral 2◊ response and showed heart support and sound responding values with his 3♡ raise. From there, all roads led to 6♡.

West led the ♠K. South, Denny Decimal, paused briefly before playing dummy's ♠7. Then he smiled and said, "Four chances!"

He took his major-suit aces at Tricks 1 and 2. When he led the ♣K to Trick 3, he held out the index finger of his left hand and said, "Chance Number One: singleton queen falling."

She didn't fall. He continued with the ♣6 and finessed the ♣J. He stuck out his middle finger and said, "Chance Number Two: club queen on side."

"Offside," said East as she won the ♣Q and returned the ♣10.

Denny stuck out his ring finger and said, "Chance Number Three: clubs three-three."

They were two-four, but hope was still alive. Denny won dummy's ♣A and led dummy's ◊5, sticking out his pinky and saying, "Chance Number Four: diamond king on side."

"Offside, said West, a former football coach called *Bear*, as he won the ◊K. "Five-yard penalty without loss of down." But of course, that was the setting trick and 6♡ was down without a tackle having been made.

In the other room, the Unlucky Expert reached 6♡ too. He won Trick 1 with the ♠A, drew trump, cashed the ♣K and ♣A, and threw his last club on dummy's ♠J, a LOL. West won and the Expert showed his hand. Plus 980.

DEAL 59. MAYBE A NEW PAIR OF EYEGLASSES

```
                        PS M'Gwire
                        ♠ void
                        ♡ K Q 9 7 5 4
                        ◊ A K 5 4
                        ♣ 6 5 3
      ♠ Q J 10 6 4                          ♠ A 8 7 5 3
      ♡ 3                                    ♡ 6
      ◊ J 9 8                                ◊ Q 10 7 6
      ♣ K J 4 2         CB M'Guff            ♣ 10 9 8
                        ♠ K 9 2
                        ♡ A J 10 8 2
                        ◊ 3 2
                        ♣ A Q 7
```

The Color-Blind Mr. M'Guff opened 1♡, and the Perpetually-Stoned Mr. M'Gwire went into his usual befuddled trance wondering what to call.

A Jacoby Forcing Raise? No, that would promise a balanced hand. A 3♠ splinter? No, that would confuse partner. Singletons being 5 or 6 times more common than voids, M'Guff would think he had one spade, not none.

Finally he settled for 2◊, which they played as forcing to game. When M'Guff bid 2♡, M'Gwire bid 4NT, Roman Keycard Blackwood. M'Guff guessed he was asking in diamonds, and replied 5♡, showing two aces without the ◊Q ... or was it without the ♡Q? Fearing a third round club loser, M'Gwire signed off in 6♡.

West led the ♠Q. M'Guff ruffed in dummy and drew trump. He cashed the ◊AK and crossruffed diamonds and spades to strip those suits. He led the ♣2 to East's ♣8, covered with the ♣9---oops, no, it was the ♣7, though he was sure he had the ♣9 when he picked up his hand.

So he finessed the ♣Q. West won the ♣K and returned the ♣2. Down one.

"Guess I need new eyeglasses," said M'Guff. Well, did he?

Yes, but he needed inner vision more. In the other room, Mrs. Guggenheim, North, never having learned any artificial forcing raises, gambled 6♡ directly over Moshe's 1♡ opening.

When West led the ♠Q, Moshe discarded dummy's ♣3, a LOL. East won the ♠A, but South's ♠K provided a second club discard. Two for the price of one! Soon Moshe claimed 6♡.

After the match, he lent M'Guff the reading glasses he kept in his shirt pocket for emergencies.

DEAL 60. A LAME EXCUSE

```
                          PS M'Gwire
                          ♠ Q 7 6
                          ♡ J 8
                          ◊ 8 5 4 2
                          ♣ K 8 5 4          SH Rose
      ♠ 10 9 8 4                             ♠ J 5 3
      ♡ K Q 10 4                             ♡ 9 7 6 5 3 2
      ◊ K J 9                                ◊ 10 6 3
      ♣ 6 3               CB M'Guff          ♣ J
                          ♠ A K 2
                          ♡ A
                          ◊ A Q 7            Willie
                          ♣ A Q 10 9 7 2
```

M'Guff and M'Gwire cut on the same team for the next match and liked each other's game well enough to play as partners again.

M'Guff opened a strong artificial and forcing 2♣ opening. He rebid 3♣ over M'Gwire's neutral 2◊ response. Fearing that M'Guff had another of his patented three-card club suits, M'Gwire bid 3NT to right-side the notrumps (as he explained in the post-mortem). M'Guff inferred that this denied as many as four cards in any suit M'Gwire could have bid at the three-level and therefore implied at least four clubs. His 6♣ jump ended the auction.

West led the ♡K. Southeast, Futile Willie, was the sitout this match. He said, "Well bid, gentleman!" when M'Gwire spread the dummy.

M'Guff won the ♡A, drew trump with the ♣A and ♣K, ruffed the ♡J in hand and cleared spades ending in dummy. When he led the ◊2 from dummy, East, Second-Hand Rose, played the ◊10. M'Guff covered with the ◊Q. West won the ◊K and returned the ◊9.

"What are you doing with that card?" said M'Guff. "I thought I had it."

Then he looked in his shirt pocket and saw Moshe's reading glasses. "Oops, I forgot to put them on."

"A lame excuse," said M'Guire. Regardless, 6♣ was down one.

"I never run out of excuses," boasted Willie. "Whenever I see my supply is running low, I manufacture a few more."

In the other room, Moshe needed neither eyeglasses nor excuses. Declaring 6♣ on a saner auction, after drawing trump he discarded the ◊7 on dummy's ♡J, a LOL.

West, Stella by Starlight, surrendered. 6♣ made.

DEAL 61. WHEN DANNY MET SALLY

```
                      ♠ J 5
                      ♡ A Q J
                      ◊ 8 5 4 2
Willie                ♣ K 8 6 3          Smug
♠ K Q 10 9 4 2                           ♠ 8 7 6 3
♡ 8 6                                    ♡ 10 9 7 4 3
◊ K 10 9                                 ◊ J 7 3
♣ 5 4                 Sally              ♣ J
                      ♠ A
                      ♡ K 5 2
                      ◊ A Q 6
                      ♣ A Q 10 9 7 2
```

When serious bridge players came to town, they often visited the Office, which was known throughout the country for its nightly team games. The newcomer introduced herself as Solid Sally from Schenectady. Danny offered to partner her when they cut one a team for the evening's first match.

Willie opened a Weak 2♠ Bid as dealer on favorable vulnerability, and Mr. Smug's two-way raise to 4♠ forced Sally to enter at the five-level. Taking Sally's self-appraisal into account, Danny raised her 5♣ to 6♣.

Willie led the ♠K to Sally's ♠A. She drew trump, led to dummy's ♡J. ruffed dummy's ♠J, cashed the ♡K and took care to cash the ◊A before crossing to dummy's ♡A to lead another diamond.

When Willie captured Sally's ◊Q with the ◊K, she turned to him and asked, "Ruff-and-sluff?"

"No, Curse of Scotland," he replied, exiting with the ◊9. "I had to have the king of diamonds for my Weak Two-Spade bid. Without it, I'd have had an obvious one-spade *psych*. My failure to psych was like the dog that didn't bark in the night."

Danny marked down one in red on his scorecard and bit his lip. Why?

In the other room, the Unlucky Expert made 6♣ by stripping only hearts and discarding the ◊6 on dummy's ♠J, a LOL play, to endplay West.

DEAL 62. TWO CHANCES OR THREE?

```
                         ♠ K J 5
                         ♡ Q 7 6 3
                         ◊ A K 6 5
Millie                   ♣ Q 8           Michael
♠ 10 4 3                                 ♠ Q 9 8 2
♡ 5                                      ♡ 8 4
◊ Q 10 8 2                               ◊ J 9
♣ J 10 9 5 3             Smug            ♣ K 7 6 4 2
                         ♠ A 7 6
                         ♡ A K J 10 9 2
                         ◊ 7 4 3
                         ♣ A
```

All roads led to a 6♡ slam and we needn't show how North got there after Mr. Smug opened 1♡. West, Thoroughly Modern Millie, led a "Jack Denies,10 or 9 shows 0 or 2 Higher" ♣J. East, Thoroughly Modern Michael, encouraged with an "Upside-Down Attitude" ♣2.

Smug won the ♣A, drew trump, and pondered his chances: a spade finesse ... or a 3-3 diamond split that would let him discard a spade and avoid a finesse.

Smug guessed to try for 3-3 diamonds first, but Millie won and exited in clubs. Smug ruffed East's ♣K, lost a spade finesse, and went down one.

"I took both chances," said Smug. But was there a third?

In the other room, Mrs. Guggenheim was on lead against 6♡. East, Futile Willie, had foisted thoroughly modern lead conventions on Googs ("Else I'll never know what she has!"). She guessed that "Jack Denies" took priority over "9 shows two higher" and led the ♣J. Good guess, Googs!

South, the Unlucky Expert, won the ♣A, two top hearts and both top diamonds. But instead of leading a third diamond, he led dummy's ♣Q to Willie's ♣K and threw the ◊7, a *LOL*. Unless East had *four* diamonds, South needed no spade finesse. The third chance came home. 6♡ made.

DEAL 63. ONE PEEK IS WORTH TWO FINESSES

```
                        ♠ K 10 6 3
                        ♡ 5 4 3
                        ◊ K 9 4
                        ♣ K 7 5
   ♠ 8                                        ♠ Q 9 7
   ♡ 10 9 8 7                                 ♡ A K 2
   ◊ Q 8 7 6 2                                ◊ J 10 5 3
   ♣ Q 10 3          Denny                    ♣ 9 6 4
                        ♠ A J 5 4 2
                        ♡ Q J 6
                        ◊ A            Bambi
                        ♣ A J 8 2
```

South, Denny Decimal, bid 4♠ over North's simple 2♠ raise. East won West's ♡10 opening lead with the ♡K and continued with the ♡A and ♡2. Denny remembered his friend Danny's Queen-Guessing Rule ("Queen of trump on the left, all other queens on the right") but he knew that it applied only to guesses. He knew the probabilities, and recited them for the benefit of Bambi, his admiring kibitzer:

"Two-two is forty percent, three-one is fifty percent, so the odds seem to be five-to-four in favor of finessing, but because there are two ways to finesse, the odds are really eight-to-five in favor of the drop."

Whereupon he led the ♠A and then low to dummy's ♠K. Alas, the ♠Q did not fall and the ♣Q was offside. 4♠ went down one.

"One peek is worth two finesses," said Bambi.

Was there any way to make 4♠ with neither peeks nor guesses?

In the other room, Moshe reached 4♠ on the same auction and the play began similarly. But Moshe unblocked the ◊A at Trick 4, led to dummy's ♠K and threw a club on dummy's ◊K. Then he ruffed a diamond, led to dummy's ♠K, and finessed the ♠J successfully.

When Bambi questioned him later, he said, "If I'd lost to a doubleton queen, West would have had to give me a ruff-sluff or come to me in clubs. Either way, I make four spades."

DEAL 64. WHAT TO ALERT

```
                    ♠ K 9 5 3
                    ♡ A K
                    ◊ 10 8 2
Moshe               ♣ Q J 8 7        Mrs. G
♠ 8 6                                ♠ 7
♡ 10 9 7                             ♡ Q 8 5 3 2
◊ K Q J 9 7 6                        ◊ 4 3
♣ K 9               Smug             ♣ 10 6 5 4 2
                    ♠ A Q J 10 4 2
                    ♡ J 6 4
                    ◊ A 5
                    ♣ A 3
```

North opened 1♣ in second seat at favorable vulnerability. South, Mr. Smug, jumped to 2♠ and asked for keys over North's 3♠ raise. On learning that both minor-suit kings were missing, he stopped in 6♠.

Moshe led the ◊K. Smug won the ◊A, drew trump ending in dummy, and let the dummy's ♣Q ride. Moshe won the ♣K and cashed the ◊J.

"Bad luck," said Mrs. Guggenheim sympathetically. "I could just as well have had the king of clubs as Moshe."

When they compared scores at the end of the match, however, they saw that South had made 6♠ in the other room. There West had opened a Weak 2◊ Bid. When it came round to him, the Unlucky Expert jumped to 3♠. North, Futile Willie, jumped to 5♠ and the Expert gambled 6♠.

However, there South placed West with the ♣K for his vulnerable Weak 2◊. Instead of taking the club finesse, he stripped the hearts and ran off the rest of his spades. In the three-card ending, West had to keep a guard for his ♣K. When he discarded the ◊Q at Trick 10, the Expert threw him in with the ◊J to lead from his ♣K. 6♠ made.

"Why didn't you open two diamonds, Moshe?" asked Smug.

"Because he and I don't play Weak Twos," said Mrs. Guggenheim.

We leave it to readers to judge: should Googs alert Moshe's passes?

DEAL 65. A "NO-COST FINESSE"?

Willie
♠ 9 7 6 2
♡ A 4
◇ A 9 8 5
♣ 5 4 3

♠ K Q 10 8 5   ♠ J 4 3
♡ Q 10 6   ♡ 9 8 5 3 2
◇ 3   ◇ 6 4
♣ K J 7 6   Denny   ♣ 10 9 8

Denny
♠ A
♡ K J 7
◇ K Q J 10 7 2   Bambi
♣ A Q 2

South, Denny Decimal, opened 1◇. West overcalled 1♠. North, Futile Willie, responded 1NT, fearing to raise a minor in case Denny had only three. After Denny jump-rebid 3◇, Willie liked his hand for slam and jumped to 4♠. Denny alerted, "Bluhmer," (don't ask!) and bid 6◇.

West led the ♠K. Denny won and drew trump. With 10 top tricks and an eleventh via a ruff in dummy, Denny took the ♡A and finessed the ♡J on the way back. He turned to his kibitzer and said, "A No-Cost Finesse. If it loses, I get to discard a club from dummy. Think I'll put the bidding and play in my new book, *1729 Things That Charlie Goren Didn't Tell you*."

West won the ♡Q and continued the ♠Q. Denny ruffed, threw a club on his ♡K, crossed to dummy's ◇A, and lost a club finesse. Down one.

"Bad luck," said Willie. "One of two finesses figured to work. 75%. Do the math!"

Well, was it bad luck? Or did South have a better play than Denny's?

In the other room, the Unlucky Expert reached 6◇ via a 2◇ raise an lots of cue bids. He won the ♠A and entered dummy in trumps twice to ruff spades. Then ♡A, ♡K, heart ruff, a LOL, ♠9 discarding the ♣2 and claimed: "Ruff-sluff or come to Papa in clubs." 6◇ made.

DEAL 66. MRS. GUGGENHEIM'S MISTAKE

```
                    ♠ J 7 2
                    ♡ 6 5 2
                    ◊ K Q 5 4
                    ♣ K 7 5
   ♠ 9 6                          ♠ 5 4
   ♡ A J 4                        ♡ Q 10 9 8
   ◊ J 10 7 3                     ◊ 9 8
   ♣ Q J 10 8      Smug           ♣ A 9 6 3 2
                    ♠ A K Q 10 8 6
                    ♡ K 7 3
                    ◊ A 6 2
                    ♣ 4
```

West led the ♣Q against 4♠ and continued the ♣10 when the ♣Q held. Mr. Smug, South, ruffed, drew trump with the ♠AK, then tried for a 3-3 diamond split. When East showed out on the third diamond, Smug hoped he had the ♡A, and led low to his ♡K.

West won the ♡A and exited in diamonds. Smug ruffed, but lost two more hearts.

4♠ went down one.

No 3-3 diamond split, both aces offside. Any way to overcome such bad luck?

In the other room, Careful Kate showed that there was a way to make 4♠. As in the Open Room, West, Post-Mortimer Snide, led and continued clubs. Kate, South, ruffed the second club with the ♠Q, led the ♠8 to dummy's ♠J, and ruffed dummy's last club with the ♠K.

She drew the rest of the defenders' trumps with the ♠A and only then did she try diamonds. When East showed out on the third diamond, she led dummy's last diamond and discarded the ♡3, *loser on loser*.

Mort won and could do no better than cash the ♡A. Kate lost only one trick in every suit but trumps and made 4♠.

Oh yes, Mrs. Guggenheim, East, got an earful from Mort: "Idiot! Why didn't you overtake my queen of clubs and return the ten of hearts?"

DEAL 67. SISTER GOLDEN HAIR'S SURPRISE

```
                    ♠ Q J 9 3
                    ♡ A 5
                    ◊ 8 5 3 2
   Moshe            ♣ 4 3 2              Kate
   ♠ 6 4                                 ♠ 7 2
   ♡ J 9 3                               ♡ Q 10 8 7 2
   ◊ A K Q 10 7                          ◊ 6 4
   ♣ K J 6          Willie               ♣ 10 9 7 5
                    ♠ A K 10 8 5
                    ♡ K 7 4
                    ◊ J 9
                    ♣ A Q 8
```

West's 2◊ overcall didn't stop Futile Willie from inviting game over North's 2♠ raise, and North accepted. Moshe, West, led the ◊K, promising the ◊Q. He continued the ◊A, completing his story, and Willie ruffed the ◊10 next.

Willie drew trump in two rounds and stripped the diamonds by ruffing dummy's ◊8. Then he stripped the hearts with the ♡AK and a ruff in dummy.

In the four-card ending, Willie led dummy's ♣2. East, Careful Kate, played the ♣9, Moshe captured Willie's ♣Q with the ♣K and returned the ♣6. Kate played the ♣10, and Willie lost a club at the end. 4♠ went down one.

Moshe smiled at Kate and said, "Your green eyes don't miss a thing."

Did Willie's blue eyes miss anything?

Yes, a loser-on-loser play. In the other room, where the Unlucky Expert bid 4♠ directly over Sister Golden Hair's 2♠ raise, he ruffed the third diamond and stripped only the hearts after drawing trump. In the *five*-card ending, he led dummy's ◊8 and discarded the ♣8.

West, Stella by Starlight, glared at the Unlucky Expert and said, "I know what you're up to. No one executes a loser-on-loser play against *me*!"

With that, Stella underplayed the ◊7. She scored her ♣K next, but 4♠ made. "Lucky, lucky!" she said as she threw her last three cards in.

"Thank God for my eight of diamonds!" said North, a former nun.

DEAL 68. THE HEART MURMUR

Millie
♠ A Q J
♡ A Q 3
◇ A Q 4
♣ A J 8 6

♠ 10 8 5 2
♡ 7 4
◇ J 9 7
♣ 7 4 3 2

♠ K 9 7
♡ K 10
◇ K 10 8 6
♣ K Q 10 9

Molly
♠ 6 4 3
♡ J 9 8 6 5 2
◇ 5 3 2
♣ 5

Thoroughly Modern Millie and Thoroughly Modern Molly were using the *Heart Murmur*, an artificial 2♡ response to an Omnibus 2♣ that denies as much as a king. Thus despite the use of transfer responses to North's 2NT rebid, South became declarer in their eventual 4♡ contract.

South lost a finesse to East's ♠K at Trick 1 and East exited passively in spades. The ♣A and a club ruff put South in his hand to take a heart finesse that lost. This time East exited passively in hearts. South won the ♡J to finesse a third time.

East captured dummy's ◇Q with his ◇K and shifted to the ♣K. Eventually, South lost another diamond; and 4♡ failed.

Any way for South to make 4♡?

Not really, unless South reads the cards almost magically, which is possible only if East huddles or shows visible signs of strength.

However, in the other room, South's neutral 2◇ response to 2♣ let North, Moshe, become declarer in 4♡ after a 2NT rebid and a Jacoby Transfer. Moshe let East's ♣K lead hold Trick 1, a LOL play of sorts.

East shifted to spades, but Moshe won the ♠Q, cashed the ♠A and exited with the ♠J to East's ♠K. East's ♣10 continuation let North make 4♡.

DEAL 69. YCMI DOUBLES AND ERKB 1430

```
                        Molly
                        ♠ 8 3 2
                        ♡ Q J 8 4
                        ◊ A J 7 5
      Willie            ♣ K 5
      ♠ K 5 4                              ♠ J 10 9
      ♡ 9                                  ♡ 6 3
      ◊ K Q 8 5 3                          ◊ 10 9 6 2
      ♣ Q 10 8 3       Millie             ♣ J 9 4 2
                        ♠ A Q 7 6
                        ♡ A K 10 7 5 2
                        ◊ void
                        ♣ A 7 6
```

Thoroughly Modern Millie alerted Thoroughly Modern Molly's 3♣ response to 1♡ as "Lillehammer," showing heart support with either 7-8 or 11-12 support points. Molly alerted Millie's 3◊ rebid as asking which. Futile Willie made one of his patented YCMI ("You Can't Make It!") doubles.

By partnership agreement, Molly's pass showed a maximum. Millie's jump to 5◊ was Exclusion Roman Keycard Blackwood. Molly's "1430" 5♠ reply showed 0 or 3 keys excluding the ◊A. Millie guessed 0 and signed off in 6♡. Got it? We're not sure that we do.

Willie led the ◊K. Millie discarded the ♠6 on dummy's ◊A and stripped both minors while drawing trump ending in dummy. In the four-card ending, she finessed the ♠Q. West won the ♠K and returned the ♠5. 6♡ went down.

Could Millie have made it?

In the other room, the Unlucky Expert reached slam via 1♡-3♡-6♡. He ruffed West's ◊K opening lead and drew trump. Then ♣K, another diamond ruff, ♣A and a club ruff in dummy. He threw the ♠6 on dummy's ◊A and the ♠7 on dummy's ◊J, a LOL play.

West won the ◊Q; unwilling to offer a ruff-sluff, West exited in spades. South won the rest. 6♡ made.

DEAL 70. MRS. GUGGENHEIM'S GOOD PLAY

```
                        ♠ A Q 2
                        ♡ 5 3 2
                        ◇ 6 4
        Willie          ♣ K 8 6 5 3        Mrs. G
        ♠ 9 8 6                            ♠ K J 10 7
        ♡ 7 4                              ♡ A 9
        ◇ Q J 9 8 5 2                      ◇ K 10 3
        ♣ 4 2            Smug              ♣ J 10 9 7
                        ♠ 5 4 3
                        ♡ K Q J 10 8 6
                        ◇ A 7
                        ♣ A Q
```

Mrs. Guggenheim, East, opened 1♣. Mr. Smug, South, overcalled 1♡. Futile Willie joined the fray with 3◇, which he insisted on playing as weak. When 3◇ came round, Smug balanced with 3♡. North shrugged and bid 4♡.

Mrs. G overtook Willie's ◇Q opening lead with the ◇K. Smug recited "Two birds with one stone," as he won the ◇A. He led the ♡K to Mrs. G's ♡A. She tried to cash the ◇10, but Willie realized that if he let her, she might lead the wrong card to the next trick, so he overtook.

He looked carefully at the spot-cards. Seeing Smug's ◇7, he inferred that Googs had the ◇3 and intended her ◇10 as suit-preference for spades, so he shifted to the ♠9.

Well done, Willie! We didn't know you had it in you. 4♡ could no longer be made. Smug lost two spade tricks and went down one.

Could Moshe, South in the other room, do better?

Moshe played Strong Single-Jump Overcalls. He jumped to 2♡ over East's 1♣. North raised to 4♡. West led the ◇Q. East, Lola, overtook and placed her palm on Moshe's thigh. Moshe smiled and ducked, saying, "Whatever Lola wants, Lola gets. You must want this trick awfully bad."

Lola played the ♡A and ♡9 to prevent a diamond ruff. Dummy's spade entry was safe from attack. Moshe unblocked clubs and dummy's ♠A was an entry to the ♣K, his tenth trick. 4♡ made.

DEAL 71. ANN BOLEYN OR JANE SEYMOUR?

```
                    ♠ Q 6 3 2
                    ♡ K J 5 4
                    ◊ Q 4 3
   Expert            ♣ 8 4            Smug
   ♠ 10 5                             ♠ A K J 8 4
   ♡ 8 7                              ♡ 6 2
   ◊ 10 9 8 6                         ◊ K J 7
   ♣ J 9 5 3 2       Henry XVIII      ♣ Q 10 7
                     ♠ 9 7
                     ♡ A Q 10 9 3
                     ◊ A 5 2
                     ♣ A K 6
```

The visitor who sat South claimed to be of royal descent from the House of Stewart. He called himself *Henry XVIII* and had names for all the queens. Vul against not, he opened 1NT. East, Mr. Smug, ventured 2♠ over North's Stayman 2♣. Henry bid 3♡ and North raised to 4♡.

West, the Unlucky Expert, led the ♠10. Henry fondled the ♠Q, said "I love you, Jane," and played dummy's ♠2. Smug followed with the ♠4. West read it as discouraging and shifted to the ◊10. Henry flung the ◊Q on the table and said, "Off with your head, Anne, you unfaithful witch!" when Smug covered with the ◊K.

Henry lost two diamonds and two spades, down one.

Could he have saved either of dummy's two queens?

In the other room South, Moshe, rated his suit-oriented hand as 19 HCP. He opened 1♡ and reached 4♡ more easily. He covered West's ♠10 opening lead with Jane (Seymour, the ♠Q?). He ruffed the third spade high, drew trump, cashed two top clubs, and ruffed a club in dummy.

He threw the ◊2 on dummy's last spade, a LOL play. East won and didn't want to offer a ruff-sluff. He shifted to the ◊7. Moshe let it ride to Anne (Boleyn, the ◊Q?) and made 4♡.

DEAL 72. JUST ONE GOOD BREAK

```
                    ♠ A Q 10
                    ♡ A K 5 3
                    ◊ A J 4 3
                    ♣ Q 8
     ♠ J 5 2                        ♠ 9 8 6 4
     ♡ 10 4                         ♡ Q J
     ◊ 2                            ◊ K 10 9 8
     ♣ K J 10 9 5 3 2   Mr. Smug   ♣ 7 6 4
                    ♠ K 7 3
                    ♡ 9 8 7 6 2
                    ◊ Q 7 6 5
                    ♣ A
```

West opened 3♣ on favorable vulnerability. North doubled. South, Mr. Smug, bid 4♡ on the strength of his 9 high-card points, five-card major and singleton club. When North raised to 5♡, Smug bid 6♡ on the strength of his 9 high-card points, five-card major and singleton club.

Smug eyed West's ◊2 opening lead suspiciously, but saw no way he could make if it were singleton, so he ducked. East won the ◊K and returned a diamond. West ruffed to beat 6♡.

Any way to make this slam despite the foul diamond split?

In the other room, East, Futile Willie, raised Mrs. Guggenheim's 3♣ preempt to 4♣ over North's double. The Unlucky Expert had ample values for his 4♡ bid, but his partner expected him to have more and raised to 6♡.

Googs led the ◊2. Had she ever underled a king against a slam? The Expert thought not. He rose with dummy's ◊A and drew trump, thanking his lucky stars for the 2-2 split. He cashed the ♣A, entered dummy in spades and led a low diamond.

East knew to duck, but South won the ◊Q, finished spades ending in dummy, and threw his ◊6 on dummy's ♣Q, a LOL play. Googs won the ♣K but had only clubs left. Her forced club return let declarer ruff in dummy and discard his last diamond. 6♡ made.

DEAL 73. SEE YOU LATER, ALLIGATOR!

(directions rotated for convenience)

```
                          Millie
                          ♠ J 7 4
                          ♡ A K
                          ◊ 7 5 4 3
        Moshe             ♣ K 8 6 3
        ♠ 10 6                              ♠ A K Q 9 8 3 2
        ♡ 9 7 6 5 4 2                       ♡ Q J 10
        ◊ Q 10 9 8                          ◊ J
        ♣ 10              Willie            ♣ 4 2
                          ♠ 5
                          ♡ 8 3
                          ◊ A K 6 2
                          ♣ A Q J 9 7 5
```

It was Board 8, the last board of the evening. Futile Willie was paired with Thoroughly Modern Millie for the first time, and she talked him into "Inverted Minor Raises" (as she called them). Willie opened 1♣ as dealer and Millie's 2♣ raise was forcing for one round. East bid 4♠ and Willie bid 5♣, not knowing whether it was an underbid, overbid or phantom save.

Millie rose from her chair and said to Willie, "Will you collect my winnings, dear? I have a late night appointment."

Willie nodded yes. Millie said, "See you later, Alligator!" and left.

East overtook West's ♠10 opening lead and tried to cash another spade, but Willie ruffed high. He drew trump, cleared the hearts, and ruffed off East's last spade honor to strip both majors. Suddenly he remembered Millie's last words. He led the ◊2, a Crocodile Coup.

Moshe eyed the ◊2 suspiciously. Could East's singleton be the ◊6?

No matter if it were! So Moshe took the ◊Q and returned the ◊8. Down one.

In the other room, the Unlucky Expert reached 5♣ after a limit raise. He ruffed the second spade, drew trump, cashed the ◊AK and dummy's ♡AK, and threw the ◊2 on the ♠J, a LOL.

East won. Sluff and ruff and 5♣ made.

DEAL 74. THE SPLINTER AND THE THORN

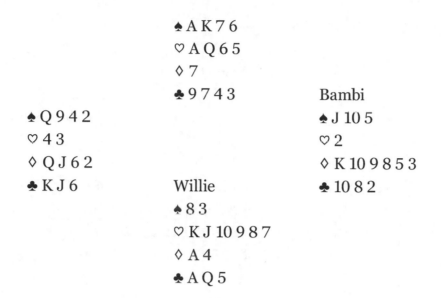

```
                    ♠ A K 7 6
                    ♡ A Q 6 5
                    ◊ 7
                    ♣ 9 7 4 3          Bambi
    ♠ Q 9 4 2                          ♠ J 10 5
    ♡ 4 3                              ♡ 2
    ◊ Q J 6 2                          ◊ K 10 9 8 5 3
    ♣ K J 6          Willie            ♣ 10 8 2
                    ♠ 8 3
                    ♡ K J 10 9 8 7
                    ◊ A 4
                    ♣ A Q 5
```

North's 4◊ "splinter" raise of his 1♡ opening left Futile Willie with no cue bids at the four-level, so he Blackwooded and guessed to stop in 6♡.

Willie captured West's ◊Q opening lead with the ◊A. He took dummy's top spades, ruffed a spade, ruffed the ◊4 in dummy, and ruffed dummy's last spade. Now he drew trump with the ♡K and dummy's ♡A.

With the hands adequately stripped, he led dummy's ♣9, intending to let it ride if not covered. Bambi, who had recently attended Denny Decimal's lecture on Surrounding Plays, smiled and covered, exclaiming "Got you surrounded!"

Willie's ♣Q lost to West's ♣K. West's ♣6 exit fetched dummy's ♣7 and Bambi's ♣8. Before capturing it with his ♣A, Willie shook a finger at the ♣8 and said, "You're a thorn in my side." West's ♣J took the setting trick to beat the slam.

But could Willie have found a way to pull the thorn?

In the other room, Moshe's "Under-and-Over" 4♣ splinter led to a 6♡ slam via cue bids. The Unlucky Expert, South, ruffed only one spade and one diamond before drawing trump ending in dummy.

When East showed out on the fourth round of spades, the Expert discarded the ♣5, a LOL, and spread his hand. "Ruff-sluff or into the big box!" 6♡ made.

DEAL 75. TWO WAYS TO STRIP TWO SUITS

```
                          ♠ 8 5
                          ♡ J 8 7 4
                          ◊ A Q 6 3
                          ♣ 7 5 4              Moshe
        ♠ J 7 4                                ♠ K Q 10 9 6 2
        ♡ 6 3                                  ♡ 5
        ◊ J 10 9 8                             ◊ 5 4 2
        ♣ A 10 9 8        Bambi                ♣ Q J 3
                          ♠ A 3
                          ♡ A K Q 10 9 2
                          ◊ K 7
                          ♣ K 6 2
```

Moshe, East, opened a Weak 2♠ Bid on favorable vulnerability. That let West sacrifice in 4♠ over Bambi's 4♡ and North took the push to 5♡.

West eschewed a spade lead in favor of the ◊J, top of his "God-given sequence" as the late great Edgar Kaplan would have called it.

Bambi had attracted two male kibitzers. She decided to put on a show for them. What normal man doesn't enjoy strip-tease?

She won the ◊K, drew trump, unblocked the ♠A, and took dummy's two remaining high diamonds to discard the ♠3. She ruffed dummy's last spade high to strip the spades, led the ♡2 to dummy, and ruffed dummy's last diamond to strip the diamonds.

In the four-card ending, Bambi had three clubs and one heart in each hand. She exited with the ♣2. Whichever defender won would have to lead clubs for her. West played the ♣8 and started to turn the trick, but Moshe overtook and returned the ♣3. Two more club tricks beat 5♡.

Could Bambi have made it?

In the other room, the Unlucky Expert, driven to the same high contract, started the play as Bambi did but stripped only the spades. In the *five*-card ending, he threw the ♣2 on dummy's last diamond. West won and had nothing better than to lead the ♣10. South's ♣K won.

He made 5♡.

DEAL 76. A DEUCE, A DEUCE, MY KINGDOM FOR A DEUCE!

                        Mrs. G
                        ♠ A Q 3
                        ♡ 5 4 3
                        ◇ A 8 7 6 4
Rose   ♣ 7 3
♠ J 9 6 2   ♠ K 8 7
♡ 8 2   ♡ 10 7
◇ Q 10   ◇ J 9 5 2
♣ J 10 9 5 4   Willie   ♣ A K 6 2
                        ♠ 10 5 4
                        ♡ A K Q J 9 6
                        ◇ K 3
                        ♣ Q 8

Mrs. Guggenheim's old-fashioned 2◇ response followed by a 3♡ raise landed Futile Willie in an iffy 4♡. West, Second-Hand Rose, led the ♣J.

East won the first two club tricks and shifted to the ♡7. Willie drew trump and set about setting up dummy's long suit. He led the ◇K followed by the ◇3. When Rose played the ◇Q on the second diamond, Willie said, "Yeah, yeah, 'Second Hand High' and all that. I read Jim and Danny's book too."

He won dummy's ◇A and ruffed East's ◇9 with the ♡Q, muttering, "Drop, jack!" When the ◇J didn't fall, he led the ♠4. Second-Hand Rose inserted the ♠9, and Willie finessed dummy's ♠Q.

East won the ♠K and returned the ♠8. Rose covered Willie's ♠10 with the ♠J, driving out dummy's ♠A. A second diamond ruff set up a trick for dummy's ◇8, but Willie couldn't get to dummy to cash it. "A deuce, a deuce, my kingdom for a deuce!" he cried as he scored 4♡ down one.

Could Willie have made 4♡ despite lacking the ♡2?

In the other room, the Unlucky Expert reached 4♡ after a forcing 1NT response followed by a raise to 3♡. But when East, Stella by Starlight, played the ◇J on the third diamond, the Expert discarded the ♠4 and listened to her chant "Lucky, Lucky!" as she threw in her cards.

4♡ made.

DEAL 77. IN HOW MANY BASKETS SHOULD YOU PUT YOUR EGGS?

```
                        Mrs. G
                        ♠ K 9 6 4
                        ♡ A 7
                        ◊ 7 6 4
        Lola            ♣ 6 5 3 2
        ♠ 5 2                               ♠ 3
        ♡ Q J 10 9                          ♡ 8 6 5 4 3 2
        ◊ K 6 3                             ◊ J 10 9 8
        ♣ J 9 8 7       Smug                ♣ Q 10
                        ♠ A Q J 10 8 7
                        ♡ K
        Danny           ◊ A Q 2
                        ♣ A K 4
```

All roads lead to the 6♠ slam that seems to hinge on a diamond finesse. Lola led the ♡Q. Danny, Southwest, smiled when he saw dummy and said, "Well bid, Googs. Nice four-heart cue bid. I'm proud of you!"

Lola frowned and whispered to Danny, "You like *her*?"

"Yes," Danny whispered back. "Looks aren't everything."

Smug won the ♡K, cashed the ♠A and led to dummy's ♠K to finish trumps. He discarded the ◊2 on the ♡A and said to Danny, "I'm not one to put all my eggs in one basket. Watch!"

"Hey, Harry," said Lola. "He's my kibitzer, not yours."

Harry (did Lola really know his name?) tried for 3-3 clubs: ♣AK and another. Lola won the ♣9 and exited with the ♣J. Smug ruffed high, led the ♠8 to dummy's ♠9, and lost a finesse of the ◊Q to Lola's ◊K. Down one. Danny whispered to Lola: "Big pickup. Jack will make it." But how?

In the other room, the Unlucky Expert declared 6♠. He won the heart lead, the ♠Q, and ♣AK. He led to dummy's ♠9 and ruffed a club. He drew the last trump with dummy's ♠K and threw the ◊2 on dummy's ♣6.

West, Stella by Starlight, said "Nobody endplays me! Lucky, lucky!"

She folded her cards and 6♠ made.

DEAL 78. GOOD SPOT CARDS

```
                    ♠ A 10 9 7
                    ♡ J 4
                    ◊ 10 8 5
                    ♣ A J 7 2          Mrs. G
    ♠ 6                                ♠ 4 2
    ♡ 8 5 3 2                          ♡ Q 10 9 6
    ◊ K 3 2                            ◊ J 9 7 4
    ♣ Q 10 9 8 3     Willie            ♣ K 6 4
                    ♠ K Q J 8 5 3
                    ♡ A K 7
                    ◊ A Q 6
                    ♣ 5
```

Futile Willie read the classic Darvas and Hart book *Right Through the Pack* for the third time and came away with a renewed appreciation of spot cards. Following North's limit raise, he fondled the ♠8, then the ♡7, then the ◊6 and finally the ♣5. Liking his spots, he decided to "trot out the old Black" as he called it.

On learning of two aces opposite, he thought briefly of asking for kings. But he realized that he needed the ◊K, not the ♣K, for 7♠ and couldn't find out which a one-king reply would show, so he settled for 6♠.

Willie won West's ♣10 opening lead in dummy, then stripped clubs and hearts to reach a four-card ending with one trump and three diamonds in each hand. Unfortunately, East, Mrs. Guggenheim, didn't know to show count and had discarded the ◊4 instead of the ◊7 on the fourth club.

So when Willie led a sly ◊5 from dummy, she had to follow with the ◊7. Willie was down one whether he ducked or covered.

Next time, Willie, have the ◊7! But could he have made 6♠ without it?

In the other room, the Unlucky Expert reached 6♠ by a different route, and the play began the same, but he took care to manage his entries. He led dummy's fourth club, the ♣J, after having ruffed his last heart in dummy.

When East showed out, he discarded the ◊6, a LOL play. West won the ♣Q but had no safe exit. He exited in diamonds, and 6♠ made.

DEAL 79. SUKI'S MISTRESS PLAY

                              Smug
                              ♠ A J 9 8 2
                              ♡ A 3 2
                              ◊ 9 7 6
        Mrs. G   ♣ Q 8   Suki
        ♠ 5 4   ♠ 6
        ♡ J 8   ♡ Q 10 9 6 4
        ◊ A K Q J 10 8 5 3   ◊ 2
        ♣ 10   Willie   ♣ K J 9 7 5 3
                              ♠ K Q 10 7 3
                              ♡ K 7 5
                              ◊ 4   Danny
                              ♣ A 6 4 2

Favorable vulnerability induced Mrs. Guggenheim to jump all the way to 5◊ over Futile Willie's third-seat 1♠ opening. Good bid, Googs, but it didn't keep North from bidding 5♠. Having second-round diamond control, Willie thought of bidding slam, but finally he passed. Good pass, Willie!

Googs led the ◊K against 5♠ and shifted to the ♣10, fetching the ♣Q, ♣K and ♣A. Good shift, Googs! Willie ruffed two diamonds to strip the suit while drawing trump. Then he crossed to dummy's ♡A and led another heart, intending to duck to West's possible doubleton honor.

Suki, the feminist bridge teacher, feared that Googs had king-low in hearts left and might go wrong if forced to win the ♡K. So she played the ♡Q. *Willie* had to win the ♡K. Suki scored the ♡9 and ♣J to beat 5♠. "Master play, Suki!" said Danny, Southeast.

"You mean *mistress* play," she replied. "Next time, say it right."

Could a master---er, *mistress*---have made 5♠?

Yes. In the other room after a similar start, Careful Kate ruffed only one diamond and made 5♠. She cashed ♡K, ♡A, and threw her last heart on dummy's ◊9, a LOL play.

West won and had to give her a sluff-ruff. Soon she claimed.

DEAL 80. BARE-NAKED LADIES

```
                        Bambi
                        ♠ K 9 7 5 4 3
                        ♡ 4 3 2
                        ◊ K J
        Moshe           ♣ 5 3          Unlucky Expert
        ♠ void                         ♠ J 2
        ♡ K Q 10 9 5                   ♡ 6
        ◊ A Q 10 7 4                   ◊ 9 8 6 5 3 2
        ♣ Q 9 2         Lola           ♣ J 10 6 4
                        ♠ A Q 10 8 6
                        ♡ A J 8 7
                        ◊ void
                        ♣ A K 8 7
```

South, Lola, opened 1♠ as dealer. West, Moshe, bid a "Pure Michaels" 2♠, which he insists on using to show the two top unbid suits unambiguously. East, the Unlucky Expert, alerted it as "reds."

Having been taught to "bid to the level of fit," Bambi, North, bid 5♠. Lola, not sure what that bid meant, bid 6♠.

Moshe led the ♡K to Lola's ♡A. Lola drew trump. She stripped the diamonds and then the clubs. In the ending she remained with ♠97 ♡64 in dummy and ♠8 ♡J87 in hand, bare in both minors in both hands.

She led the ♡4 from dummy and said, "Hey, Jack, got the queen of hearts for the Queen of your Heart?"

Jack blushed and said, "Sorry, I have only diamonds." Moshe took two heart tricks. Down one.

Lola says she gets whatever she wants. Any way she could have gotten one more trick without putting her hand on Moshe's thigh?

Yes. In the other room, Careful Kate also reached 6♠. Instead of ruffing her last club in dummy, she threw the ♡3. East won but his forced diamond exit let Kate ruff in hand while discarding dummy's ♡4. 6♠ made.

DEAL 81. THE GOOD SACRIFICE

```
                        ♠ 8 7 5
                        ♡ 8 7 3 2
                        ◇ 3
                        ♣ A J 10 7 3
        ♠ A Q 4                           ♠ J 10 9 6
        ♡ Q J 10 9 6                      ♡ K 5 4
        ◇ Q J 8 5                         ◇ K 9 7 4 2
        ♣ Q              Willie           ♣ 4
                        ♠ K 3 2
                        ♡ A
                        ◇ A 10 6
                        ♣ K 9 8 6 5 2
```

South, Futile Willie, opened 1♣. West doubled, North, Mr. Smug, raised to 4♣, and East strained to bid 4◇. This spurred South to bid 5♣. Surprisingly for our era's undisciplined bidders, the auction ended there.

West led a "surprise" ♡Q, which rode to Willie's ♡A. He drew trump with dummy's ♣A and ruffed a heart. He cashed the ◇A and ruffed a diamond in dummy. He ruffed a second heart. He ruffed his last diamond in dummy. He ruffed dummy's last heart.

Having stripped the red suits in the 5-card ending he had reached,, he crossed to dummy's ♣10. He led the ♠8 from dummy, covered by the ♠9. and …curtains, down one.

"Good save, Willie," said Smug. "They're cold for four diamonds. we win two IMPs!

Well, did they?

Not exactly. In the other room, where the Unlucky Expert was South, Mrs. Guggenheim put him in 5♣ voluntarily ("You play them so well, dear!").

He began to strip the red suits as Willie did, but when East showed out on dummy's last heart, he discarded the ♠2, a LOL. West won but could take only one more spade trick. 5♣ made. Smug and Willie lost 10 IMPs.

DEAL 82. THIS TIME IT'S A PHANTOM

```
              ♠ J 7 5
              ♡ K 6
              ◇ A 9 6 4 3
              ♣ 7 5 4
♠ 6 4                            ♠ 9
♡ A J 8 7 2                      ♡ Q 10 9 5 4 3
◇ J 5                            ◇ Q 10 8
♣ A K J 6     Willie             ♣ 10 9 2
              ♠ A K Q 10 8 3 2
              ♡ void
              ◇ K 7 2
              ♣ Q 8 3
```

It's futile to try to shut Futile Willie out, as East may have learned after raising West's non-vul 1♡ opening to 4♡. Willie thought he might have a vulnerable game, and he bid 4♠.

Playing Patriarch Opening Leads, in which a king-lead normally shows the queen, West led the ♣A but shifted to the ♠6 when East played a discouraging ♣2.

Willie won with dummy's ♠J and led the ◇3, intending to cover East's card. When East played the ◇8, Willie won the ◇K and drew the last trump with his ♠A. The ◇2 brought forth West's ◇J, which Willie let hold.

Alas, East overtook with the ◇Q, returned the ♣10, and two more club tricks sank the contract.

"Another good save," said Willie, marking -100 on his scorecard.

"I'm afraid not," said Smug. "This time it's a phantom. We can beat four hearts. Lose four IMPs."

Was Mr. Smug right?

No. In the other room, Moshe, facing the same defense in 4♠, threw his ♠8 under dummy's ♠J at Trick 2 and discarded the ◇2 on dummy's ♡K at Trick 3, a LOL. West won and exited in trump. Moshe won, ruffed dummy's diamonds good, and made an overtrick.

Plus 650, and a 13-IMP pickup.

DEAL 83. "NICE TRY, NO LUCK"

Mrs. G
- ♠ A 5
- ♡ Q 10 9 2
- ♢ A K 8 3
- ♣ 7 5 2

West
- ♠ J 10 9 6 2
- ♡ 7
- ♢ J 9 5 4
- ♣ K J 6

East
- ♠ K Q 8 7 3
- ♡ 5 4
- ♢ 7 6
- ♣ 10 9 8 3

Smug
- ♠ 4
- ♡ A K J 8 6 3
- ♢ Q 10 2
- ♣ A Q 4

An artificial forcing heart raise and some adroit cue-bidding put South, Mr. Smug, at the helm in 6♡. He won the opening spade lead in dummy and drew trump. Then he "tried all his chances," first to drop a singleton or doubleton ♢J, next for a 3-3 diamond split, and when that didn't materialize, a club finesse. That too failed.

"Nice try, no luck," said Mrs. Guggenheim sympathetically.

Did the Unlucky Expert have any better luck in 6♡ in the other room?

Well, yes. Luckily, he thought to ruff a spade after winning dummy's ♠A at Trick 1. Luckily, he was able to draw trump in fewer than three rounds. Luckily, when diamonds split, it was West rather than East who held the master diamond.

Luckily, he lost track of the diamonds and thought dummy's ♢8 was high, for he said "discarding the club four on the good eight of diamonds," and claimed.

"What's good about it?" asked Stella by Starlight, West.

Luckily, Stella did not say, "Lucky, lucky," for by now we were all tired of hearing it.

DEAL 84. TWO WAYS TO STROKE THE CAT

```
                        Mort
                        ♠ 10 8 7 4
                        ♡ 9 7 6 4
                        ◊ A K
    Mrs. G              ♣ A 6 4              Willie
    ♠ Q J 6                                  ♠ void
    ♡ K Q 5 3                                ♡ A J 10 8 2
    ◊ 9 6 4                                  ◊ Q 8 5 3
    ♣ 9 7 3             Lola                 ♣ K Q J 2
                        ♠ A K 9 5 3 2
                        ♡ void
                        ◊ J 10 7 2           Danny
                        ♣ 10 8 5
```

Lola, South, reached 4♠ after Willie opened 1♡. Googs, West, led the ♡K. Willie whispered to Danny, Southeast, "I'll bet she misplays it!" "I heard that," said Lola, as North put down the dummy.

"But Danny slipped me a draft of his book on LOL plays and I can make one here." "Don't forget Jim's huge contribution, sweetheart," said Danny.

"Whatever," said Lola. She ruffed, cashed dummy's ◊AK, and came to her hand with the ♠A. Then she led the ◊J to discard dummy's ♣4, exclaiming "Loser on Loser!" as Willie won the ◊Q. East shifted to the ♣K, driving out dummy's ♣A.

Lola returned to her hand with the ♠K, smiled, and said, "I read their book on Entries too." She discarded dummy's last club on the ◊10 and lost only to Mrs. G's ♠Q.

Making five. "Well played, dearie," said North, Pre-Mortimer Snide, the first kind words anyone remembered him saying. "A wash," he added. "The Unlucky Expert will be stroking the cat in the other room. He's never missed a loser-on-loser play in his life."

Was Pre-Mortimer Snide right?

No. There West, Mr. Smug, doubled 4♠. The Unlucky Expert ruffed four hearts in hand and a diamond in dummy while taking five top tricks. At Trick 11 he led the ◊J ensuring a trick for dummy's ♠10.

Plus 690, *six* IMPs

CHAPTER FIVE

DANGER HANDS AND L - O - L

DEAL 85. AN UNUSUAL DUCK

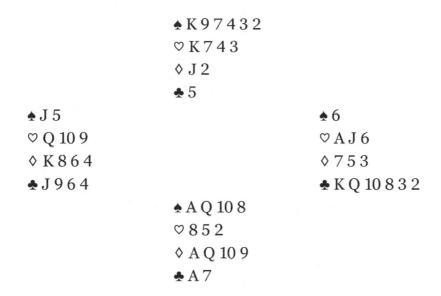

♠ K 9 7 4 3 2
♡ K 7 4 3
♢ J 2
♣ 5

♠ J 5
♡ Q 10 9
♢ K 8 6 4
♣ J 9 6 4

♠ 6
♡ A J 6
♢ 7 5 3
♣ K Q 10 8 3 2

♠ A Q 10 8
♡ 8 5 2
♢ A Q 10 9
♣ A 7

South opened 1NT and North bid 2♣, Stayman. East doubled and South bid 2♠, showing, by partnership agreement, both four spades and a club stopper. He would have passed without a club stopper. North raised to 4♠ and West led the ♣4.

Declarer won Trick 1 and drew trumps. The red suits were menacing but if the diamond finesse was on, declarer might discard some of dummy's hearts. Declarer tried the diamond finesse. West won the ♢K and shifted to a heart. Down one, losing three hearts and one diamond.

Unlucky? Both finesses offside but in the other room, declarer made four spades. How?

That declarer played for both finesses to lose. She ducked East's ♣Q in order to discard a diamond from dummy on the ♣A. East shifted to a diamond. Declarer went up with her ace, discarded dummy's other diamond, and kept West, the danger hand, off lead by taking a ruffing finesse through West's ♢K. West had no winning option.

If he covered, declarer would ruff and have two high diamonds to discard hearts. If West ducked, declarer would keep discarding hearts. And if East had the ♢K? Same result, the heart king was safe. Making four spades, losing two hearts and one club.

DEAL 86. ANOTHER DANGER HAND

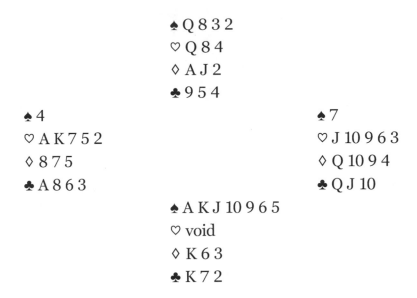

```
                    ♠ Q 8 3 2
                    ♡ Q 8 4
                    ◊ A J 2
                    ♣ 9 5 4
  ♠ 4                                ♠ 7
  ♡ A K 7 5 2                        ♡ J 10 9 6 3
  ◊ 8 7 5                            ◊ Q 10 9 4
  ♣ A 8 6 3                          ♣ Q J 10
                    ♠ A K J 10 9 6 5
                    ♡ void
                    ◊ K 6 3
                    ♣ K 7 2
```

West opened 1♡. East's preemptive jump to 4♡ did not keep South from ending the auction by bidding 4♠. West led the ♡A.

Declarer ruffed the opening lead and drew the two outstanding trumps. Having never met a finesse she didn't like, she led a diamond to the jack. East won and the shift to the ♣Q meant down one. Sure, swift, and wrong.

"Didn't you read Dr J's book on the finesse only as a last resort," asked North, marking minus 50 in her scorecard.

How did the declarer in the other room find her way home?

At Trick 1, instead of ruffing, declarer discarded a diamond, so that East, the danger hand, could never get in with the ◊Q to lead a club through."

West shifted to a diamond, won by South's king. Declarer played a spade to dummy's eight and ruffed another heart. Then she cashed the ◊A, ruffed dummy's last diamond and went to dummy with another trump.

Now another loser-on-loser play, the ♡Q, discarding a club. West was endplayed and could do no better than cash the ♣A.

North marked down plus 420.

DEAL 87. A SECOND SUIT TO AVOID A DANGER HAND

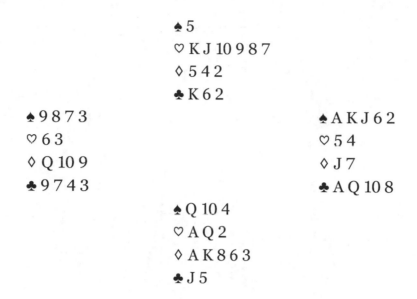

```
                    ♠ 5
                    ♡ K J 10 9 8 7
                    ◊ 5 4 2
                    ♣ K 6 2
    ♠ 9 8 7 3                        ♠ A K J 6 2
    ♡ 6 3                            ♡ 5 4
    ◊ Q 10 9                         ◊ J 7
    ♣ 9 7 4 3                        ♣ A Q 10 8
                    ♠ Q 10 4
                    ♡ A Q 2
                    ◊ A K 8 6 3
                    ♣ J 5
```

East opened 1♠ and South overcalled 1NT. Playing Texas Transfers in reply to 1NT overcalls, North bid 4◊ to insist on game in his long heart suit. West led the ♠9 against the 4♡ contract.

East won and shifted to the ◊7 (a better shift than the ◊J). Declarer drew trumps and cashed the other high diamond, then a third diamond hoping East would have to win this trick. Not today – West won the ◊Q and shifted to a club. Down one.

Wrong operation and the patient died. Could you have saved the patient?

In the other room, declarer also saw a second suit but also saw the danger of West leading a club. After winning the first diamond, he led the ♠Q and discarded a diamond, a LOL play. But notice the difference.

East won but could not attack clubs. South could set up the diamonds with one ruff, not letting a defender obtain the lead again. After drawing trumps ending in his hand, declarer had two good diamonds to discard two clubs from dummy.

He lost two spades and one club, making four hearts.

DEAL 88. THE SAME FROM THE OTHER SIDE

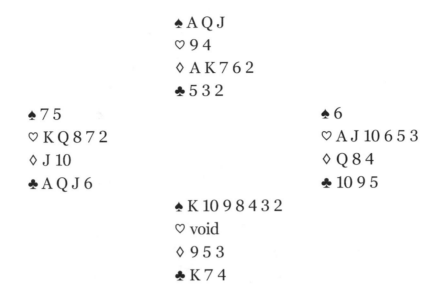

♠ A Q J
♡ 9 4
◇ A K 7 6 2
♣ 5 3 2

♠ 7 5
♡ K Q 8 7 2
◇ J 10
♣ A Q J 6

♠ 6
♡ A J 10 6 5 3
◇ Q 8 4
♣ 10 9 5

♠ K 10 9 8 4 3 2
♡ void
◇ 9 5 3
♣ K 7 4

With no one vulnerable, South opened 3♠ and North raised to 4♠. West led the ♡K, East encouraged and declarer ruffed. After drawing trumps, declarer tried to set up the diamonds, but East won the third diamond and shifted to a club.

Declarer lost three club tricks, down one.

Poorly played but was he punished?

In the other room, instead of ruffing at Trick 1, he discarded a diamond so he could set up dummy's diamonds without letting East in to shift to clubs. Did this plan work?

It would have, but he never got to execute it, for this East was alert. Instead of encouraging at Trick 1, she overtook partner's opening lead of the ♡K with her ♡A.

Now declarer had no winning option. If he discarded, here comes a club. So he ruffed and hoped West would win the third diamond.

Again- not today. Down one. A pushed board, no justice.

DEAL 89. SECOND SUIT AND DANGER HAND

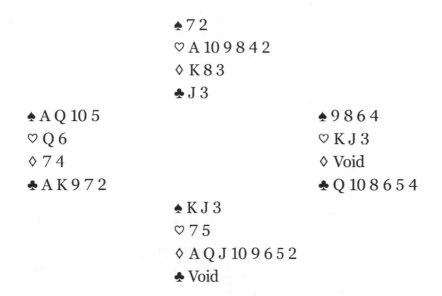

♠ 7 2
♡ A 10 9 8 4 2
◊ K 8 3
♣ J 3

♠ A Q 10 5
♡ Q 6
◊ 7 4
♣ A K 9 7 2

♠ 9 8 6 4
♡ K J 3
◊ Void
♣ Q 10 8 6 5 4

♠ K J 3
♡ 7 5
◊ A Q J 10 9 6 5 2
♣ Void

With both sides vulnerable, North opened a Weak Two Heart bid, East passed and South bid what he thought he could make- 5◊. West's double ended the auction, although with the fortunate spade position, East-West could make 6♣.

West led the ♣K and declarer ruffed. After drawing trumps, declarer had no way to keep East from obtaining the lead in hearts. The spades shift meant down one.

Was there a road to making the contract?

In the other room, declarer discarded a heart from her hand at Trick 1, allowing West to remain on lead. By discarding a card she had to lose anyhow, she kept East, the danger hand, from getting in.

With plenty of entries, it was easy now to set up the heart suit to discard the spade losers. The best West could do was cash the ♠A to prevent an overtrick.

DEAL 90. A TWO FOR ONE TRADE

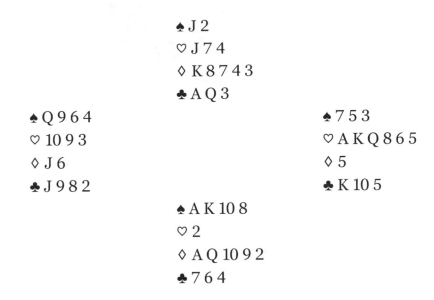

```
                        ♠ J 2
                        ♡ J 7 4
                        ◊ K 8 7 4 3
                        ♣ A Q 3
        ♠ Q 9 6 4                       ♠ 7 5 3
        ♡ 10 9 3                        ♡ A K Q 8 6 5
        ◊ J 6                           ◊ 5
        ♣ J 9 8 2                       ♣ K 10 5
                        ♠ A K 10 8
                        ♡ 2
                        ◊ A Q 10 9 2
                        ♣ 7 6 4
```

After East opened 1♡ and South made a take-out double, North-South reached a pushy 5◊ contract. West led the ♡10. South, anxious to avoid a club shift, covered with dummy's ♡J.

East won and continued hearts, ruffed by South.

Declarer drew trumps and lost a club finesse. He still had another club loser at the end for down one.

Was there a way to avoid those club losers?

Make a trade. In the other room, after drawing trumps ending in the dummy, declarer led the ♠J, not really caring if it won or lost. West won the queen and switched to a club. But declarer was in control, having made a good trade.

He rose with the ♣A and discarded two of dummy's clubs on his good spades.

Making 5◊, losing only one spade and one heart.

DEAL 91. ENDPLAY THE DEFENDER
WITH THE HIGH CARDS

```
                    ♠ K 9 6 3
                    ♡ A 10 3
                    ◊ 7 2
                    ♣ A 7 6 4
♠ 5                                      ♠ 10 4
♡ K Q J 9 5 2                            ♡ 8 6
◊ A Q 5 3                                ◊ J 10 9 6 4
♣ 9 5                                    ♣ Q J 10 3
                    ♠ A Q J 8 7 2
                    ♡ 7 4
                    ◊ K 8
                    ♣ K 8 2
```

South opened 1♠ and West overcalled 2♡. When North cue bid showing a limit raise or better with spades, South bid game.

West led the ♡K. Declarer won the ace and drew trumps. Hoping to duck a club to West, the safe hand, he led a club from dummy.

But East played the ♣10. Curtains- there was no way to avoid losing one heart, two diamonds, and one club. Down one.

How did the declarer in the other room avoid the 'danger'?

Play started the same in the other room. But after drawing trumps, declarer cashed first the ace, then the king of clubs and led a heart. West won and played a third heart.

However, declarer discarded his club loser on the third heart. West was finished. Declarer now lost only two hearts and one diamond.

Another heart would have given declarer a ruff-sluff.

DEAL 92. KEEPING THE DANGER HAND OFF LEAD

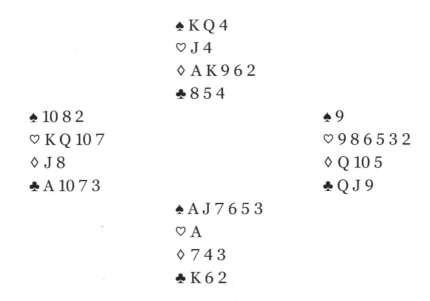

```
              ♠ K Q 4
              ♡ J 4
              ◇ A K 9 6 2
              ♣ 8 5 4
♠ 10 8 2                        ♠ 9
♡ K Q 10 7                      ♡ 9 8 6 5 3 2
◇ J 8                           ◇ Q 10 5
♣ A 10 7 3                      ♣ Q J 9
              ♠ A J 7 6 5 3
              ♡ A
              ◇ 7 4 3
              ♣ K 6 2
```

South opened 1♠ and North bid 2◇, game forcing in their methods, and later raised spades.

West led the ♡K against 4♠. The contract was always safe if East had the club ace, but declarer saw an extra chance; set up the diamonds and perhaps West would have to win the third diamond.

Some days it doesn't pay to get up. After drawing trumps, declarer first tried the diamonds, but East won the third diamond. Then when West had the club ace, declarer was down one, losing three clubs and one diamond.

Unlucky, yes. But was there a better line of play declarer overlooked?

In the other room at Trick 2, declarer crossed to the ♠K and played the ♡J, discarding a low diamond. This loser-on-loser play put the 'safe' hand, West, back on lead. What could West do?

When declarer regained the lead, he cashed the ace of trumps, then was able to set up the diamonds without letting the opponents regain the lead. The trump queen was the entry to the good diamonds.

DEAL 93. GOOD DEFENSE BUT NO
CIGAR; A SIMILAR PLAY

```
                    ♠ K Q 3
                    ♡ J 9 7
                    ◊ 6 4
                    ♣ A 7 6 3 2
    ♠ 10                              ♠ J 9
    ♡ A K 10 8 5                      ♡ Q 6 4 3
    ◊ A Q 10 9 2                      ◊ J 8 7 3
    ♣ 10 5                            ♣ Q J 9
                    ♠ A 8 7 6 5 4 2
                    ♡ 2
                    ◊ K 5
                    ♣ K 8 4
```

Despite West opening 1♡ and making a game try by bidding 3◊, spades won out as usual, North-South reaching 4♠. West led the ♡A, but did not make the lazy continuance of the ♡K.

He knew this would have allowed declarer to discard a club, a LOL play. West shifted to a trump at Trick 2.

Declarer won in dummy, playing low from his hand. He led the ♡9, but East alertly covered with the queen, trying to get on lead for a diamond switch. Declarer ruffed and played another trump to dummy. When he led the heart jack and discarded a club, West was forced to win.

West exited a club. Declarer won the club king, led to the club ace, and ruffed a club establishing the club suit. Declarer went to dummy and........

Oh, oh? Please don't tell me you wasted your deuce of trumps at Trick 2?

How are you going to get to the dummy?

DEAL 94. SETTING THE STAGE

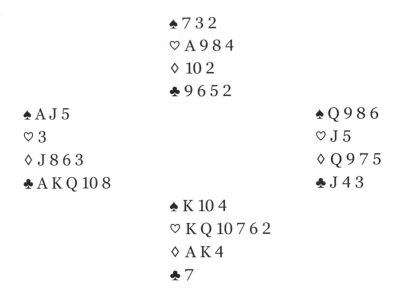

```
                    ♠ 7 3 2
                    ♡ A 9 8 4
                    ◇ 10 2
                    ♣ 9 6 5 2
    ♠ A J 5                       ♠ Q 9 8 6
    ♡ 3                           ♡ J 5
    ◇ J 8 6 3                     ◇ Q 9 7 5
    ♣ A K Q 10 8                  ♣ J 4 3
                    ♠ K 10 4
                    ♡ K Q 10 7 6 2
                    ◇ A K 4
                    ♣ 7
```

South opened 1♡ and West overcalled 2♣. Playing Weak Single-Jump Raises, North bid 3♡ and South bid game. West started with two top clubs and declarer ruffed the second round.

After drawing trumps, South played the A-K of diamonds and ruffed a diamond.

He then tried a spade to his ten. West won the jack and played another high club. Declarer still had two spade losers. Down one.

Almost but not quite. Could you have done better?

In the other room, after ruffing Trick 2, declarer played the king, then ace of trumps and ruffed another club. He cashed the A-K of diamonds and ruffed a diamond. Now the stage was set.

But instead of a spade, he played the last club and discarded a spade loser. West won and looked around, but he was toast. A minor card would result in a ruff-sluff and a spade would present declarer with a spade trick.

Making four hearts, losing two clubs and one spade.

DEAL 95. PUNCH AND COUNTERPUNCH

```
                    ♠ J 9 5
                    ♡ A K J 7
                    ◇ 4 3
                    ♣ A 10 9 8
    ♠ A 4                              ♠ 2
    ♡ 10                               ♡ 8 6 4 3
    ◇ A J 10 6 5                       ◇ K Q 9 8 7
    ♣ K Q J 5 2                        ♣ 6 4 3
                    ♠ K Q 10 8 7 6 3
                    ♡ Q 9 5 2
                    ◇ 2
                    ♣ 7
```

West opened 1◇ and North made a take-out double. Things heated up as East jumped preemptively to 4◇. South bid a hopeful 4♠, but of course was pushed to 5♠ by West.

The ♣K was a promising opening lead, but with trump control West led his singleton ♡10.

His devious plan was to win the first round of trumps and hopefully underlead in diamonds to East to get a heart ruff. His devious plan succeeded. Down one.

Was this play duplicated in the other room?

West in the other room had the same idea. He led his singleton which declarer won. Recognizing the opening lead as a likely singleton, this declarer had a devious plot of his own.

Before touching trumps, he played the ♣A and led another club, discarding his singleton diamond. When West won the first trump, he was 'cut off' from East, unable to reach his partner to get the heart ruff he so longed for.

Another nicely played 'Scissors Coup', cutting the link between the defenders' hands.

Notice that if West held a club card higher than the ten, he could have foiled this coup by playing second hand high.

DEAL 96. AVOIDING DANGER

```
                    ♠ A Q J
                    ♡ Q J 8
                    ◊ J 10 7 5
                    ♣ 9 7 4
    ♠ 10 9 8 7                      ♠ K 4 3 2
    ♡ 6                             ♡ 7 5 2
    ◊ Q 6 4 3                       ◊ 9 8 2
    ♣ A 6 3 2                       ♣ Q J 10
                    ♠ 6 5
                    ♡ A K 10 9 4 3
                    ◊ A K
                    ♣ K 8 5
```

South opened 1♡ and North bid 1NT, which they played as forcing, preparatory to inviting game in hearts with good three-card support. South bid game and West led the ♠10.

Declarer took the spade finesse into the danger hand and the hand was over quickly. East won the spade king and switched to the ♣Q. The defense took the first four tricks.

"Really partner," asked North, "Have you ever met a finesse you didn't like?"

Was there a way to stay out of danger?

In the other room, declarer did not want to take any chances, and also had more respect for some spot cards. She won the ♠A at Trick 1 and cashed the A-K of diamonds. She crossed to the ♡8 and led the ◊J, not really caring what East played.

If East covered, declarer would ruff and the ◊10 would be the tenth trick. If East didn't cover, declarer would discard a spade. West could win and lead another diamond.

East would ruff and declarer would overruff. Then back to dummy with a trump to take a ruffing finesse with the ♠Q.

Game, set, and match!

DEAL 97. DIAGNOSING TROUBLE

```
                      ♠ A Q 9 6
                      ♡ A Q 2
                      ◇ 7 4 3
                      ♣ A J 9
   ♠ 7 3 2                              ♠ K 8 5 4
   ♡ 5 4                                ♡ 3
   ◇ A Q 8 6                            ◇ J 10 9
   ♣ K 10 8 7                          ♣ Q 5 4 3 2
                      ♠ J 10
                      ♡ K J 10 9 8 7 6
                      ◇ K 5 2
                      ♣ 6
```

North raised South's 3♡ opening to 4♡ and West led a trump. Viewing the hand as a second suit type hand, declarer drew trumps and attempted to set up the spades to discard losers. Wrong operation – when East won the spade king, the diamond shift meant down one quickly.

Was there a different operation available for this patient, I mean contract?

In the other room, declarer diagnosed a 'danger' hand. He won the opening lead in hand and led his singleton club. He had two plans:

Plan A – if West played low, he would win the ace and return the nine. If then East played low he would discard the ♠10, a loser-on-loser play. Then if West won and returned another trump, he would win and cash the ♠A. Now he would lead the ♠Q for a ruffing finesse, pitching a diamond if East played low. The ♠9 would be the tenth trick.

Plan B – If East covered the ♣9, ruff and lead a trump to dummy. Then try the ♣J, again throwing the spade unless East covered. If East held both the ten and a high club honor, he would have to try a 'normal' spade finesse as a last resort.

If West played the ♣K on the first club play, he would duck. Anything but letting East get on lead for the fatal diamond shift.

DEAL 98. TRANSPORTATION PROBLEMS

```
                         ♠ A K 4
                         ♡ K J
                         ◊ J 10 7
                         ♣ A 8 7 6 2
  ♠ void                                    ♠ J 10 9 8 7 6 5
  ♡ A 7 4 2                                 ♡ 6
  ◊ A K Q 5 4                               ◊ 8 3 2
  ♣ J 10 9 5                                ♣ K Q
                         ♠ Q 3 2
                         ♡ Q 10 9 8 5 3
                         ◊ 9 6
                         ♣ 4 3
```

North opened 1NT and East took advantage of the favorable vulnerability to overcall 2♠. South bid 2NT, the Lebensohl convention, forcing North to bid 3♣. South's subsequent 3♡ bid was weak, ending the auction. West led the ◊A and (not best) continued with the diamond king and queen.

Declarer ruffed the third round and started the trumps. West won the second round with the ace and shifted to a club. Declarer was stuck in the dummy. If he played ace and a club, East would win and give West a spade ruff. If he tried to reach his hand with a spade, same result. Down one.

How did the declarer in the other room find his way back?

After the same start, at Trick 3 the other declarer discarded a club rather than ruff the third diamond. This LOL play served the purpose of keeping East, the danger hand from obtaining the lead before all the trumps were drawn.

Declarer lost three diamonds and one trump. Making three hearts

DEAL 99. ENDPLAY THE DANGER HANDS' PARTNER

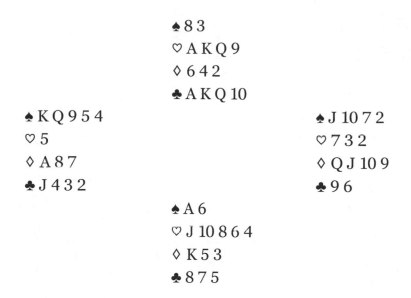

```
              ♠ 8 3
              ♡ A K Q 9
              ◇ 6 4 2
              ♣ A K Q 10
♠ K Q 9 5 4                    ♠ J 10 7 2
♡ 5                            ♡ 7 3 2
◇ A 8 7                        ◇ Q J 10 9
♣ J 4 3 2                      ♣ 9 6
              ♠ A 6
              ♡ J 10 8 6 4
              ◇ K 5 3
              ♣ 8 7 5
```

After a 1♣ opening and a 1♡ response, West's 1♠ butt-in didn't shut out North's jump raise to 3♡. South bid 4♡. West led the spade king and East played the jack. Declarer won the ace and drew trumps.

How to play the club suit? From the top or take a finesse? Since he didn't want East in to lead a diamond, he cashed the three top clubs. OK, not dead yet; he played dummy's last club and discarded a diamond, smiling at West, a LOL play he had recently learned from a book he had bought.

Unfortunately, the smile didn't last long. West played a low spade to East's ten of spades. The diamond switch meant down one.

Another case of a good operation but the patient dying.

Malpractice? Call a lawyer? Do we need a different doctor?

In the other room, declarer made a better play by ducking Trick 1, keeping the danger hand off lead. The rest of the play was the same except when declarer made his LOL play, West could no longer reach East. The best he could do was cash the diamond ace.

This patient survived the operation. Making four hearts.

DEAL 100. A PAR IS A PAR

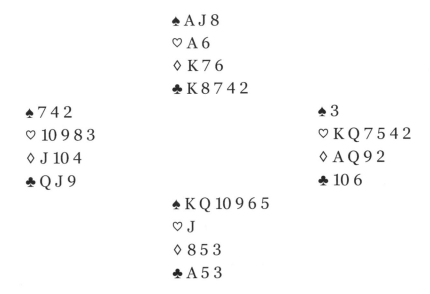

♠ A J 8
♥ A 6
♦ K 7 6
♣ K 8 7 4 2

♠ 7 4 2
♥ 10 9 8 3
♦ J 10 4
♣ Q J 9

♠ 3
♥ K Q 7 5 4 2
♦ A Q 9 2
♣ 10 6

♠ K Q 10 9 6 5
♥ J
♦ 8 5 3
♣ A 5 3

South opened 2♠ and North raised to 4♠. West led the ♥10. Declarer won the ace and drew trumps. The obvious source of tricks was to set up the club suit.

Declarer was unable to duck a club to East, West always covering South's club card. When West obtained the lead in clubs, the switch to the diamond jack meant down one, losing one club and three diamonds.

How did the declarer survive and make four spades in the other room?

Again, it's like golf. It's not how, but how many. No one asks you how you made par. The same in bridge. The declarer in the other room ducked the opening lead, playing the ♥6. East had to overtake at Trick 1 to prevent South from winning with the jack.

East returned a heart. Declarer won the ace, discarding a club from hand. Then she cashed the trump ace.

With clubs splitting 3-2, it was possible to set them up with one ruff. She drew the remaining trumps with dummy's K-J and discarded two diamond losers on the good clubs. Even if clubs were 4-1, the fifth club could be established.

Making five spades, losing one heart and one diamond. A par is a par.

DEAL 101. GOING LOW

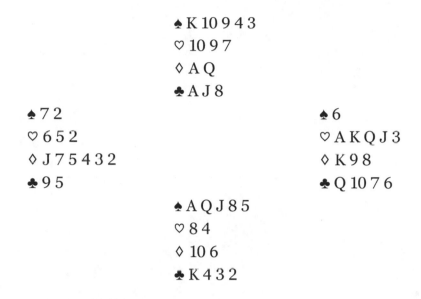

```
                    ♠ K 10 9 4 3
                    ♡ 10 9 7
                    ◇ A Q
                    ♣ A J 8
    ♠ 7 2                              ♠ 6
    ♡ 6 5 2                            ♡ A K Q J 3
    ◇ J 7 5 4 3 2                      ◇ K 9 8
    ♣ 9 5                              ♣ Q 10 7 6
                    ♠ A Q J 8 5
                    ♡ 8 4
                    ◇ 10 6
                    ♣ K 4 3 2
```

At equal vulnerability, East opened 1♡ and South overcalled 1♠. North bid 4♠. West led the ♡2 and East played three rounds of hearts.

Declarer ruffed the third round high and drew trumps. He played a club to the jack, losing to West's queen. West returned a low club. With clubs dividing 4-1, South needed the diamond finesse. Down one.

Was there a way to avoid the diamond finesse?

In the other room, at Trick 6, declarer led a low club. When West played low, declarer played low, the eight. Had West played the club nine, declarer would have played the jack, just trying to lose a trick to the 'safe' hand. In either case, East had no winning return.

Making four spades.

CHAPTER SIX

A LOT OF THIS,
A LITTLE OF THAT

DEAL 102. PLEASE, PARTNER, MAKE YOUR CONTRACT

                         ♠ void
                         ♡ A 7 6 2
                         ◇ K 8 4 2
                         ♣ A 9 4 3 2
    ♠ Q J 8   ♠ A 10 9 7 6 4 3 2
    ♡ 4   ♡ 9 8
    ◇ Q 10 9 7   ◇ 5
    ♣ Q 10 8 7 6   ♣ K J
                         ♠ K 5
                         ♡ K Q J 10 5 3
                         ◇ A J 6 3
                         ♣ 5

At favorable vulnerability, East opened 4♠. South overcalled 5♡ and West bid 5♠. North was certainly bidding at least 6♡. Would 6♣ be a cue bid or might it lead to trouble? He settled for 6♡. West led the ♠Q.

"Might have missed seven," said South seeing the dummy. North, having heard this before, thought "please, just make your contract. I'll be happy."

Declarer ruffed the opening lead. Setting up the clubs seemed reasonable but that plan quickly proved unsuccessful. And when West showed up with ◇Q1094, declarer had two unavoidable diamond losers. Down one.

"Partner, you were in six, not seven. What was the problem?" asked North.

At the other table, declarer claimed after the same opening lead. How?

The opening lead was unfortunate for the defense. At Trick 1, declarer announced he was making a LOL play, discarding a diamond from dummy while at the same time making his spade king high. That would take care of the other diamond loser.

The rest were all high. Making six hearts, thank you.

115

DEAL 103. A REPEATING THEME

```
                      ♠ void
                      ♡ Q J 10 5 2
                      ◇ A 9 6 5 3
                      ♣ 5 4 2
  ♠ Q J 10 5                              ♠ A 9 7 6 3 2
  ♡ 8                                     ♡ 7 3
  ◇ Q 10 7 4 2                            ◇ K J 8
  ♣ K J 3                                 ♣ 10 8
                      ♠ K 8 4
                      ♡ A K 9 6 4
                      ◇ void
                      ♣ A Q 9 7 6
```

South opened 1♡ and North bid 4♡, a weak raise usually with lots of trumps and distribution, but not a lot of HCP. South was not deterred from one slam try, 5♣, so North thought "Well, OK, I've got extras too" and bid 6♡.

West led the ♠Q and declarer ruffed in dummy. The ♣AQ9 was a 'good' holding but he could not first eliminate all the diamonds and spades. After drawing trumps, he tried a club to his nine and later a club to his queen.

Not his day. Down one.

"Partner, we just went thru this," moaned North. "Will you ever get it right?"

Was it a better day for the declarer in the other room?

The other declarer did not get distracted by his club holding and was not in love with finesses. He discarded a club from dummy at Trick 1 and another club on the spade king. Then he set up the clubs with ruffs in dummy.

No finesses, thank you. Making six hearts.

DEAL 104. ONE MORE LOOK

```
                    ♠ A K 10 6 2
                    ♡ void
                    ♢ 8 5 3
                    ♣ J 10 6 4 3
♠ 9 3                                        ♠ J 8 7 5 4
♡ Q J 10 9 6 5 2                             ♡ A 8 7 3
♢ K                                          ♢ Q 10 6 2
♣ 8 7 5                                      ♣ void
                    ♠ Q
                    ♡ K 4
                    ♢ A J 9 7 4
                    ♣ A K Q 9 2
```

South opened 1♢. West preempted 3♥. North-South played "Negative Doubles" through 4♠, so North doubled to show spades and appropriate values, but East pushed on to 4♡.

South bid 5♣. North had to make a good guess and raised to 6♣. West led the ♡Q.

When South ruffed the first trick, you could almost hear North wanting to scream "No, you are in six, not seven!"

With suits not breaking friendly, declarer could not find twelve tricks.

How was the other declarer able to claim at Trick 2?

At Trick 1, in the other room, declarer discarded a diamond from dummy. With his spade king now high to take care of the other diamond loser, unless West could ruff diamonds or spades, South had the rest.

DEAL 105. RENDER UNTO CAESAR

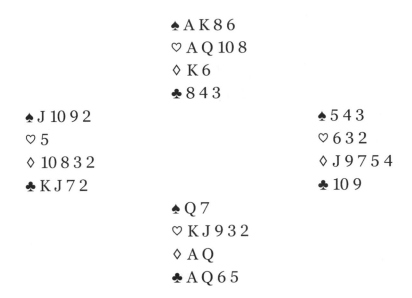

          ♠ A K 8 6
          ♡ A Q 10 8
          ◊ K 6
          ♣ 8 4 3

♠ J 10 9 2   ♠ 5 4 3
♡ 5   ♡ 6 3 2
◊ 10 8 3 2   ◊ J 9 7 5 4
♣ K J 7 2   ♣ 10 9

          ♠ Q 7
          ♡ K J 9 3 2
          ◊ A Q
          ♣ A Q 6 5

South opened 1♡ and North bid 2NT to show a balanced forcing raise. South rebid 3♥ showing no shortness, but not a complete minimum. North-South had agreed to play Kickback, an improvement upon Roman Keycard Blackwood when hearts are trump. After a series of artificial bids, N-S landed in 6♥.

"For a full explanation, endorse next year's income tax refund check and mail it to Danny, who will spend three days writing you one."

West led the ♠J. Declarer knew he could discard one club loser on a high spade. He drew trumps and couldn't resist taking a club finesse. Down one, losing two club tricks.

"Is there ever a finesse you don't take," asked an exasperated North? "I have a book you have to read, or we are not playing again."

How did the other declarer make the slam with no finesses?

Render unto Caesar what is Caesar's. After drawing trump, South cashed two high diamonds and discarded one club on a high spade. As the play thus far suggested, West had the master spade. South threw him in with it pitching another club, a LOL play.

West won and had to lead up to South's remaining ♣AQ. or give declarer a ruff/sluff.

Making six spades.

DEAL 106. BREAKING COMMUNICATIONS

```
                          ♠ A Q J 3
                          ♡ 7 5 4
                          ◊ J 10 9 4 3
                          ♣ A
     ♠ 9 8 2                              ♠ K 10 7 6
     ♡ K Q J 10 3                         ♡ 9 2
     ◊ 5                                  ◊ 6 2
     ♣ K J 7 6                            ♣ Q 10 8 5 3
                          ♠ 5 4
                          ♡ A 8 6
                          ◊ A K Q 8 7
                          ♣ 9 4 2
```

South opened 1◊ and West overcalled 1♡. North's "Negative Double" that conventionally showed four spades after West's 1♡ overcall fetched a sensible 2◊ rebid from South. The pair dodged the 3NT bullet when North jumped to 5◊. West led the ♡K.

Declarer won and drew trumps. He led a spade to dummy's queen losing to East's king. The heart return meant down one.

"Now what?" asked South, seeing North just grimacing as she marked minus 50.

Why was North grimacing? How would you have played?

In the other room, the bidding and opening lead were the same. The bidding suggested West had only five hearts; no weak jump overcall, no heart rebid, so declarer ducked the opening lead, perhaps losing a trick but thinking it might come back.

West continued hearts and declarer won the second heart as East followed. But after drawing trumps and taking the losing spade finesse, East did not have heart to return. Declarer discarded his other heart loser on the good spade.

Making five diamonds. "Very nice," said North, marking plus 400.

DEAL 107. HIDDEN ASSETS

$$\spadesuit \text{A K 6 2}$$
$$\heartsuit \text{J 9 8 3}$$
$$\diamond \text{6 4 3}$$
$$\clubsuit \text{5 4}$$

$$\spadesuit \text{9} \qquad\qquad \spadesuit \text{8}$$
$$\heartsuit \text{A K 10 5} \qquad \heartsuit \text{7 6 4 2}$$
$$\diamond \text{K J 7} \qquad\qquad \diamond \text{10 9 5 2}$$
$$\clubsuit \text{10 9 7 6 3} \qquad \clubsuit \text{K Q 8 2}$$

$$\spadesuit \text{Q J 10 7 5 4 3}$$
$$\heartsuit \text{Q}$$
$$\diamond \text{A Q 8}$$
$$\clubsuit \text{A J}$$

South opened 1♠ and West doubled. North bid 3♠, a "Mixed Raise" which North-South conventionally played as a good raise, 7-9 HCP and four trumps. South bid game. West led the ♡A and switched to the ♣10.

Declarer won the ace and drew trumps. Faced with four possible losers, he played another club trying to endplay West. But East won the trick and shifted to a diamond.

Declarer finished down one.

There were hidden assets. Could you have put them to use?

In the other room, declarer was paying closer attention to the spot cards. Trick 1 consisted of the ace and queen of hearts. South won the club shift and led to dummy's ♠K to draw trump. Then he led dummy's ♡J and threw the ♣J, saying, 'When you can't follow suit, follow rank.'

West won the ♡K to continue clubs. South ruffed, crossed to dummy in trump and led the ♡8, following rank again with the ◇8.

LOL # 1. Declarer discarded his club loser on the heart as West won the trick. West played a club and declarer ruffed. Back to the dummy with a trump and here came another heart.

LOL # 2 as declarer discarded a diamond. The last heart in dummy, the nine was high and declarer had a trump entry. His diamond loser was going away.

He lost three heart tricks, making four spades.

DEAL 108. A SIMILAR THEME

```
                    ♠ 8
                    ♡ Q J 10 9 4
                    ◇ A 5 2
                    ♣ Q 9 8 7
♠ A 6                                    ♠ K J 10 9 7
♡ 8 5                                    ♡ 7 2
◇ Q 10 8 7 3                             ◇ J 9
♣ 10 6 4 2                               ♣ A K 5 3
                    ♠ Q 5 4 3 2
                    ♡ A K 6 3
                    ◇ K 6 4
                    ♣ J
```

South opened 1♠ and rebid 2♡ after North's forcing 1NT which they played as forcing. When North raised hearts, South bid game. West led the ♣2. East won and switched to a trump. Declarer led a spade, planning for a cross-ruff.

The defense won and played another trump. Declarer finished with nine tricks: Two high diamonds, two high hearts, and five ruffs.

Down one.

Do you see a better line of play?

In the other room, declarer won Trick 2 in the dummy and led the queen of clubs. This was covered by the ace and ruffed high. Now declarer gave up a spade. West won and returned a trump.

Declarer won in dummy and led the nine of clubs, discarding a diamond loser from his hand. West won the ten, but this was the third and last trick for the defense.

Dummy's last club was high, and declarer could ruff his diamond loser.

Ten tricks.

DEAL 109. SPOT CARDS, THOSE LOVELY SPOT CARDS

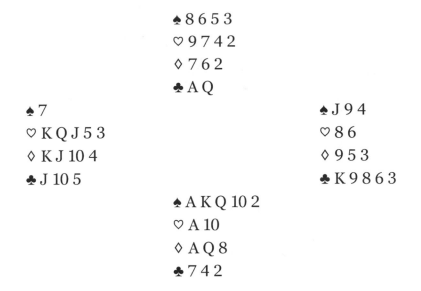

```
                         ♠ 8 6 5 3
                         ♡ 9 7 4 2
                         ◇ 7 6 2
                         ♣ A Q
         ♠ 7                              ♠ J 9 4
         ♡ K Q J 5 3                      ♡ 8 6
         ◇ K J 10 4                       ◇ 9 5 3
         ♣ J 10 5                         ♣ K 9 8 6 3
                         ♠ A K Q 10 2
                         ♡ A 10
                         ◇ A Q 8
                         ♣ 7 4 2
```

South opened 1♠ and West made a 2♡ overcall. When North raised spades, South bid game. West led the ♡K, East following with the ♡8, likely a doubleton.

Being finesse addicted, declarer confidently led a club to the queen, losing to East's king. East returned a diamond and of course that finesse was doomed. Declarer still had another heart loser and a diamond loser. Down one.

"Partner, did you ever read 'Finesses, The Last Resort'?" asked North.

What was North referring to? Was there a better line of play?

Maybe a tad unlucky; the club finesse was a favorite based on the bidding, but finesses do not always win. The other declarer had read that book and was more focused on the heart spots.

After drawing trumps, she led the heart ten losing to the jack. This left West with the ♡Q53 and dummy with ♡97.

West switched to a club. Declarer won the ace and led another heart, discarding a diamond. West won and led a club to East's king. Declarer won the diamond return with her ace and ruffed a club to reach dummy.

The ♡7 was waiting with a smile. ☺ Away went a diamond loser.

Making four spades, no finesses. Thank you, Dr J.

DEAL 110. THE VALUE OF VOIDS

```
                    ♠ A 10 7 4
                    ♡ A 9 2
                    ◊ K 9 2
                    ♣ K Q J
    ♠ 6                             ♠ 5 2
    ♡ Q J 10 4                      ♡ 8 7 5
    ◊ J 8                           ◊ Q 10 7 5
    ♣ A 9 8 7 5 4                   ♣ 10 6 3 2
                    ♠ K Q J 9 8 3
                    ♡ K 6 3
                    ◊ A 6 4 3
                    ♣ void
```

South opened 1♠ and North bid 2NT, which they played as a Jacoby Forcing Raise. South bid 3♣, by agreement a singleton or void. North bid 3◊, a cue bid showing the ◊A or ◊K. South bid 4♣, showing first-round club control. North's 4♡ bid showed the ♡A or ♡K.

South trusted North not to have given value to the ♣A if he had it, since he would know it was facing a void that South had shown by his 4♣ bid. If both partners have first round control of a suit, that's an extreme case of duplication of values. So he bid 6♠. West led the ♡Q.

South's thinking was 'up-side' down. He tried for 3-3 diamonds to discard his heart loser. When diamonds were 4-2, he lost a heart and a diamond.

There was a much easier line of play. By now I'm sure you see it, no?

Marty Bergen always says, "I love voids." Declarer won the opening lead in the other room and drew trumps. He led the club king discarding a heart. West won, but now declarer simply discarded the two diamond losers on the ♣QJ.

Making six spades Yes, with isolated honors, like Kxx or KJx opposite shortness, you should devalue your hand. But with a more solid sequence like the one above, KQJ can prove useful as we have just seen.

DEAL 111. WHICH SUIT?

```
                    ♠ K Q 2
                    ♡ 8 6
                    ◇ Q 9 6 4 3 2
                    ♣ 7 4
♠ 7                                      ♠ J 10 4
♡ K Q J 10 9 2                           ♡ 7 4
◇ A J 8                                  ◇ K 10
♣ K 10 6                                 ♣ Q J 8 5 3 2
                    ♠ A 9 8 6 5 3
                    ♡ A 5 3
                    ◇ 7 5
                    ♣ A 9
```

West opened 1♡ and East bid a forcing 1NT. South bid 2♠. West persisted with 3♡, but as usual spades won as North ended the auction with 3♠.

West led the ♡K.

Declarer counted eight tricks. One heart ruff would fulfill his contract, so he won the opening lead and played a heart back. He ruffed the next heart high, knowing East was likely out of hearts. But when he drew trumps and East turned up with ♠J104, declarer had an unexpected trump loser. Nine became eight. Down one.

How can declarer assure nine tricks?

Right game plan, wrong execution. In the other room, play was the same for the first two tricks. But at Trick 3, when West returned another high heart, this declarer discarded his club loser from dummy.

Now he could obtain his ruff, just in a different suit. He ruffed a club low, preserving the high trumps.

Nine stayed nine. Making three spades.

DEAL 112. GOOD DAYS, BAD DAYS

```
                    ♠ Q 8 7 5 3 2
                    ♡ void
                    ◊ A 7 5 3
                    ♣ A 6 3
  ♠ 9                                   ♠ 6
  ♡ K 8 4                               ♡ A 7 6 5 3 2
  ◊ K Q J 10 9 8                        ◊ 6 2
  ♣ 10 9 8                              ♣ K Q J 4
                    ♠ A K J 10 4
                    ♡ Q J 10 9
                    ◊ 4
                    ♣ 7 5 2
```

Vul against non-vul opponents, South opened 1♠ and West, taking advantage of the favorable vulnerability, bid 4◊. "That's just great," thought North.

He bid 6♠. West decided there was probably no future in diamonds and led a club.

"Great bid, great lead," said East, marking plus 100 in his scorecard.

And how did their teammates do in the other room?

North-South also reached 6♠ on a slightly calmer auction. West led the ◊K. This gave declarer a chance. Do you see how?

Again, spot cards. Declarer knew West did not have the ♡AK, no heart lead. If the two top heart honors were divided, there was hope. He drew the two trumps and led the ♡Q, discarding a club. East won and returned a club.

Declarer won and came to his hand. Taking a ruffing finesse now against West in hearts, the slam rolled home.

"Well done, partner," said North marking plus 1430.

```
                        ♠ Q J 10 9
                        ♡ Q 8 7 4
                        ◇ A
                        ♣ 9 8 3 2
        ♠ K 8 6 5 3                         ♠ A 7 4 2
        ♡ A 2                               ♡ 6
        ◇ J 10 2                            ◇ K Q 8 5 3
        ♣ J 10 5                            ♣ K Q 4
                        ♠ void
                        ♡ K J 10 9 5 3
                        ◇ 9 7 6 4
                        ♣ A 7 6
```

East opened 1◇ and South overcalled 1♡. Another hearts versus spades battle. North tried to defend 4♠ doubled but right or wrong, South pulled to 5♡, doubled by West who led the ◇J.

Declarer won the ace and played a trump. West won and switched to a club. Declarer lost two club tricks, down one.

"We survived your opening lead," said East.

What did East mean? Could declarer make the contract after that lead?

In the other room, the contract and opening lead were the same. But having just seen the previous deal, declarer recognized this was the same theme seen from the other side of the table.

He won the ◇A and led the spade queen. If East covered, he would ruff, return to dummy and lead the spade jack, discarding a club. Or the other way around if East ducked the first spade. Either way, the LOL meant making five hearts doubled.

"Sorry," said West. "If I lead a club or a heart they are going down."

DEAL 114. WOW

♠ K 10 7 5 4
♡ Q 4
◇ A 8 7 4
♣ 10 9

♠ 2   ♠ Q J 9 6 3
♡ 8 7 3   ♡ A
◇ Q J 6 3 2   ◇ K 10 9 5
♣ K 8 5 4   ♣ A 7 2

♠ A 8
♡ K J 10 9 6 5 2
◇ void
♣ Q J 6 3

East opened 1♠ and South overcalled 2♡, maybe somewhat conservative. When North bid 2NT, South bid 4♡. West led the ♠2.

Declarer, maybe thinking about what was for dinner instead of keeping his eye on the ball, won the spade ace and started the trumps. East won the first round and gave West a spade ruff. Big surprise. Down one, with two club losers next.

"Partner, pay attention. You are so cheap," said North.

Cheap? What did North mean? What could declarer do?

In the other room, in the same contract, declarer was paying attention. He won the opening lead with dummy's spade king and played the diamond ace, discarding..... the ace of spades.

An ace for an ace.

Should we call this a WOW play, a winner-on-winner? Having performed a spectacular Scissors Coup, it was now safe to draw trumps, losing one heart and two clubs.

DEAL 115. DO IT AGAIN!

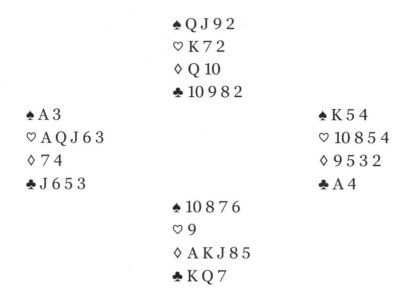

♠ Q J 9 2
♡ K 7 2
◇ Q 10
♣ 10 9 8 2

♠ A 3
♡ A Q J 6 3
◇ 7 4
♣ J 6 5 3

♠ K 5 4
♡ 10 8 5 4
◇ 9 5 3 2
♣ A 4

♠ 10 8 7 6
♡ 9
◇ A K J 8 5
♣ K Q 7

South opened 1◇ and West overcalled 1♡. North-South were playing the usual version of Negative Doubles, in which a double of a 1♡ overcall is a surrogate for a 1♠ response with exactly four spades.

It was another hearts versus spades fight, everyone bidding maybe a little too much.

When the smoke cleared, South was declaring 3♠. West led the ♡A and East played the four.

West switched to a club. East won the club ace and returned a club. When declarer started the trumps, West jumped up with his ace to give East a club ruff. Down one.

"Partner, don't you ever learn from your mistakes," asked North?

What did North mean? How should South have played?

At the other table, play went the same for the first three tricks. But seeing the approaching danger, South saw the cure. She led a diamond to dummy's queen.

Then she played the heart king, discarding the club king, another WOW play to be able to overruff if necessary.

Making three spades. A winner-on-winner!

DEAL 116. DISCARD, DON'T RUFF

```
                    ♠ 9 7 6 5 4 3 2
                    ♡ 6 4
                    ◊ K 2
                    ♣ 5 4
   ♠ A K 8                              ♠ Q J 10
   ♡ Q 10 9 8                           ♡ K J 7 3 2
   ◊ 10 9 8 7                           ◊ Q J
   ♣ 10 9                               ♣ 8 7 6
                    ♠ void
                    ♡ A 5
                    ◊ A 6 5 4 3
                    ♣ A K Q J 3 2
```

After somehow missing a laydown 3NT, North-South arrived in 5♣. West led the ♠A, ruffed by declarer. Declarer cashed the A-K of diamonds as both defenders followed. He ruffed a third diamond, overruffed by East.

East returned a trump. Declarer still had to lose a diamond and a heart. Down one.

Would you have found a way to eleven tricks?

In the other room, declarer also cashed the A-K of diamonds. But when he led a third diamond and West covered, declarer discarded his heart loser from dummy, a LOL play. Now he could not be prevented from ruffing a heart in the dummy.

If West persisted with a fourth diamond, declarer could discard another heart.

He lost two diamonds, making five clubs.

DEAL 117. BLIND SPOT

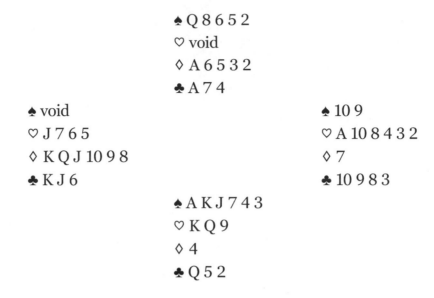

♠ Q 8 6 5 2
♡ void
♢ A 6 5 3 2
♣ A 7 4

♠ void　　　　　　　　　　　♠ 10 9
♡ J 7 6 5　　　　　　　　　♡ A 10 8 4 3 2
♢ K Q J 10 9 8　　　　　　♢ 7
♣ K J 6　　　　　　　　　　♣ 10 9 8 3

♠ A K J 7 4 3
♡ K Q 9
♢ 4
♣ Q 5 2

South opened 1♠ and West bid 2♢. North's 3♢ cue bid showed a limit raise or better in spades. South bid 4♦ which showed a diamond control but at least two fast club losers. North's 4♡ showed a control in the other two suits, hearts and clubs, else he would have signed off in 4♠. South bid 4NT, Roman Keycard Blackwood. North's 5NT reply showed two aces and a useful void. South gambled 6♠.

West led the ♢K. Declarer won and worried about the club suit. If the club king was with East, he would lose only one trick. He drew trumps and led a low club towards his queen. Down one, losing two clubs.

"Partner, did you have a blind spot?" asked North.

What did North mean? How would you have played the slam?

In the other room, North also cue-bid 3♢. When South jumped to 4♠, North gambled 6♠.

Declarer was not worried about the clubs. This declarer simply led the heart king. If covered, he could ruff in dummy and later discard a club from dummy on the heart queen.

And if not covered, he could discard a club anyhow, with the same result.

Making six spades.

DEAL 118. UNFORTUNATE LEAD?

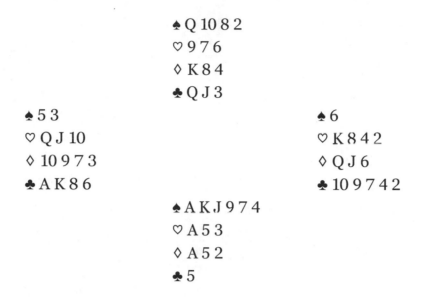

♠ Q 10 8 2
♡ 9 7 6
◊ K 8 4
♣ Q J 3

♠ 5 3
♡ Q J 10
◊ 10 9 7 3
♣ A K 8 6

♠ 6
♡ K 8 4 2
◊ Q J 6
♣ 10 9 7 4 2

♠ A K J 9 7 4
♡ A 5 3
◊ A 5 2
♣ 5

South opened 1♠ and North bid 2♠, South bid 4♠ and West led the ♡Q.

Declarer ducked one round but had four losers with nowhere to go.

Down one. When comparing with her teammates after the session, she found the other declarer had made four spades.

Can you see how the declarer in the other room made 4♠?

In the other room, West led the ♣A, then switched to the ♡Q. After drawing trumps, declarer led the queen of clubs and discarded a heart.

He still had another heart loser but was able to discard the diamond loser on the now established jack of clubs. He lost only two clubs and one heart.

What would you have led? The 'normal' looking lead of the club ace was unfortunate for the defense, and conversely fortunate for the declarer.

DEAL 119. AN IMP IS AN IMP

```
                        ♠ J 10 6 2
                        ♡ J 10 6
                        ◇ 9 2
                        ♣ Q J 6 5
        ♠ void                              ♠ Q 9 5 4
        ♡ A Q 9 4                           ♡ K 3
        ◇ K J 10 8 3                        ◇ 7 6 5
        ♣ A K 3 2                           ♣ 10 9 8 4
                        ♠ A K 8 7 3
                        ♡ 8 7 5 2
                        ◇ A Q 4
                        ♣ 7
```

With East-West vulnerable, South opened 1♠ and West doubled. North bid 2♠. After doubling 1♠ for takeout, West acted again when North's simple 2♠ raise came back to him. Having shown support for the other suits, West bid his five-card diamond suit, and South took the push to 3♠.

West led the ♣A like he had done on the previous board and there it was again; the Q-J combination. Unsure of how to continue, West shifted to a low heart.

East won the heart king and returned the suit to West's A-Q. West played a fourth heart. Declarer ruffed high, but East overruffed and returned a club. Declarer ruffed in hand and could take the diamond ace. But that was down three. Minus 150.

How did the comparison go with his teammates?

In the other room, declarer also played 3♠ undoubled. But he was only down two. When West led the fourth heart, he realized ruffing was pointless; East was certainly going to overruff and the diamond finesse was doomed.

Declarer discarded a diamond from dummy instead of ruffing. He held the result to down two, minus 100.

DEAL 120. FORCING A WINNER

```
                          ♠ A Q 5
                          ♡ Q J 7
                          ◊ 9 8 5 3
                          ♣ A J 10
        ♠ 7 2                              ♠ 8 4
        ♡ A K 8 5 4                        ♡ 10 9 6 3 2
        ◊ A Q 10                           ◊ J 4
        ♣ 9 6 2                            ♣ K Q 8 5
                          ♠ K J 10 9 6 3
                          ♡ void
                          ◊ K 7 6 2
                          ♣ 7 4 3
```

North opened 1♣ and South responded 1♠. West bid 2♥. North doubled. North-South were playing a convention called Support Doubles, in which North's double of West's 2♡ Overcall showed three spades and said nothing else about his hand. East raised to 3♡, but South's 3♠ ended the auction. West led the ♡A. Declarer ruffed and counted seven top tricks.

One more might come from a long diamond, and a double club finesse offered a 75% chance. At Trick 2 he played a club to dummy's ten losing to the queen. He played low on the diamond return. West exited a club and declarer repeated the finesse with the same result.

The long diamond came home, the club did not. Down one.

Did declarer at the other table find that elusive ninth trick?

Yes, by force rather than finessing. The opening lead was the same ♡A. South counted seven top tricks. After ruffing the ♡A at Trick 1, he drew trump and used dummy's remaining ♡QJ to drive out West's ♡K, an LOL play, setting up an eighth trick. Eventually, a fourth-round diamond trick became his ninth trick.

Making three spades, losing one heart, three diamonds, and no clubs. Those ace leads from AKxx have not been working out very well on these past few hands. Doesn't it seem dummy always has QJx(x)?

DEAL 121. WATCH THOSE SPOTS

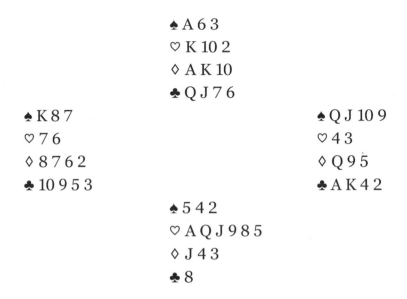

♠ A 6 3
♡ K 10 2
◇ A K 10
♣ Q J 7 6

♠ K 8 7
♡ 7 6
◇ 8 7 6 2
♣ 10 9 5 3

♠ Q J 10 9
♡ 4 3
◇ Q 9 5
♣ A K 4 2

♠ 5 4 2
♡ A Q J 9 8 5
◇ J 4 3
♣ 8

South opened 2♡, a Weak Two Bid and North bid 4♡.

West led the ♣10; jack, king, eight. East shifted to the ♠Q. Declarer won the ace and drew trumps. He took a diamond finesse. East won the queen and the defense cashed two rounds of spades. Down one.

"Another finesse you couldn't resist, partner," asked North?

Was there a line of play to avoid the finesse?

In the other room, declarer was paying more attention to the spot cards, especially the clubs. Dummy had ♣Q76 with only the ace and nine outstanding.

He drew trumps ending in dummy and led the ♣Q covered by the ace (if not, he could discard a spade and claim; he knew RHO had the ace from Trick 1).

He ruffed the club ace and went to dummy with a diamond. He led another club from ♣76.

One might describe a LOL play as a "ruffing finesse that loses." Declarer had reached that position against the club nine. A loser was going away, now or later.

Making four hearts.

DEAL 122. TWO KINGS - TWO CHOICES?

```
                    ♠ A Q J 6
                    ♡ 7 5
                    ◊ K Q 10 7 5 3
                    ♣ 5
        ♠ 10 8 7 4                      ♠ K 9 3 2
        ♡ Q 10 6 4                      ♡ K J 9 8 3
        ◊ 6 4                           ◊ 9 8 2
        ♣ K 4 2                         ♣ 8
                    ♠ 5
                    ♡ A 2
                    ◊ A J
                    ♣ A Q J 10 9 7 6 3
```

South open 1♣, North bid 1◊, South bid 3♣, invitational, perhaps a bit of an underbid but without many choices. When North accepted game with his 3♠ bid, South gambled 6♣. More often than most bidding theorists imagine, good bidding consists of good gambles.

West led a heart, the best lead for the defense. Declarer, missing two significant kings, took a spade finesse first, hoping to discard his heart loser.

He finished down two, losing one spade, one heart, and a club.

Sure, swift, and wrong.

Was this all just a guess? Which was the proper line of play?

In the other room, declarer wanted to increase his chances. There was a line of play that if wrong at least kept him alive. He led a spade to the ace at Trick 2 and then led the spade queen.

If East had the king and covered, his problem was solved. When the queen wasn't covered, he discarded his heart loser. If it lost, he had the trump finesse in reserve.

Yes. A ruffing finesse that fails is a Loser-on-Loser play that works.

Making six clubs, losing only one club trick.

DEAL 123. STRIP'EM AND STUFF'EM

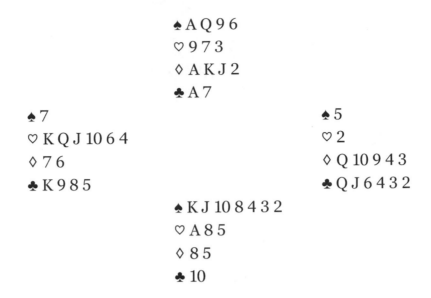

```
                      ♠ A Q 9 6
                      ♡ 9 7 3
                      ◇ A K J 2
                      ♣ A 7
  ♠ 7                                      ♠ 5
  ♡ K Q J 10 6 4                           ♡ 2
  ◇ 7 6                                     ◇ Q 10 9 4 3
  ♣ K 9 8 5                                 ♣ Q J 6 4 3 2
                      ♠ K J 10 8 4 3 2
                      ♡ A 8 5
                      ◇ 8 5
                      ♣ 10
```

West opened a Weak Two Heart bid and North doubled. When South jumped to 4♠, North optimistically bid 5♠, asking South if he had a heart control to bid a slam. South bid 6♡, showing first round control of hearts, but North was happy to settle for 6♠. West led the ♡K.

Declarer won, drew the two outstanding trumps and tried a diamond finesse to shed a heart loser. East won the queen and returned a club. South lost a heart in the end.

Down one. "Little pushy, don't you think," asked South? "How could you go down?" retorted North.

How did the declarer in the other room bring home the "pushy" slam?

In the other room, South won the same opening lead, drew trumps, cashed the club ace and ruffed a club. He cashed the ◇AK and ruffed a diamond, finishing the 'strip'. Then he went to dummy with a trump and led the ◇J, discarding a heart, the LOL play, the 'stuff'.

East won and had to concede a ruff-sluff as the second heart loser disappeared.

Making six spades. No finesses, thank you.

DEAL 124. AGAINST THE ODDS

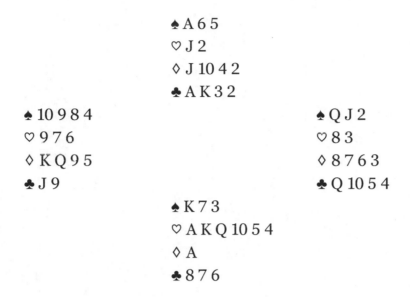

♠ A 6 5
♡ J 2
◇ J 10 4 2
♣ A K 3 2

♠ 10 9 8 4
♡ 9 7 6
◇ K Q 9 5
♣ J 9

♠ Q J 2
♡ 8 3
◇ 8 7 6 3
♣ Q 10 5 4

♠ K 7 3
♡ A K Q 10 5 4
◇ A
♣ 8 7 6

South opened 1♡ and North bid 2♣, playing Two-Over-One game forcing. South rebid 3♡, an unnecessary jump conventionally setting trumps. North bid 3♠, a cue bid for hearts.

South bid a waiting 3NT, hoping North could cue bid 4♣. Just what the doctor ordered. After North's 4♣, South asked for Key Cards and bid 6♡.

West led the ◇K (rightly or wrongly) and declarer won the ace. With a potential loser in both black suits, declarer tried to set up the clubs by ducking one round and playing for a 3-3 split.

Not today, and not most days.

Down one.

Do you see a better line of play? A 3-3 division is against the odds.

In the other room, West also led the ◇K. After drawing trumps, declarer played the jack of diamonds and discarded a club, a LOL play. Later West followed low helplessly while South discarded a spade on dummy's ten of diamonds and claimed his slam.

Making six hearts. Unlucky opening lead? You decide.

DEAL 125. BUY A BOOK

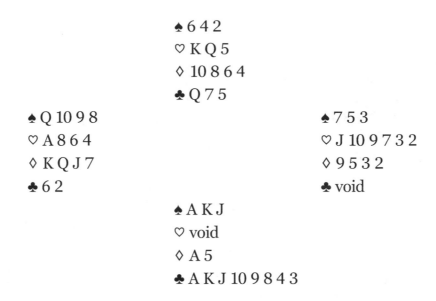

```
                    ♠ 6 4 2
                    ♡ K Q 5
                    ◊ 10 8 6 4
                    ♣ Q 7 5
♠ Q 10 9 8                          ♠ 7 5 3
♡ A 8 6 4                           ♡ J 10 9 7 3 2
◊ K Q J 7                           ◊ 9 5 3 2
♣ 6 2                               ♣ void
                    ♠ A K J
                    ♡ void
                    ◊ A 5
                    ♣ A K J 10 9 8 4 3
```

South opened 2♣, artificial and strong and rebid 3♣ after North's 2◊ waiting bid. When North bid 4♣, South decided 6♣ was high enough. West led the ◊K.

Declarer won with his ace, cashed the spade ace and drew trumps. Being a finesse addict, he went to dummy and took a spade finesse.

Down one. Declarer must have had a blind spot and only five fingers on each hand.

"I have to get you to read Dr J's book about avoiding finesses," said an unhappy North, marking minus 50 in her scorecard.

How did the play go in the other room?

The declarer in the other room was Mordecai Twelve-Fingered Brown. He had read the book. He went to dummy with a trump and led the heart king. When East played low, declarer discarded his losing diamond. West won the ace. Declarer later discarded the spade jack on the heart queen.

"It's a good thing I made you read that book," said North smiling as she marked down plus 920. "Your two extra fingers sure came in handy on this deal," said North as the pair exchanged 'High Sixes'."

DEAL 126. INTERMEDIATES COUNT TOO

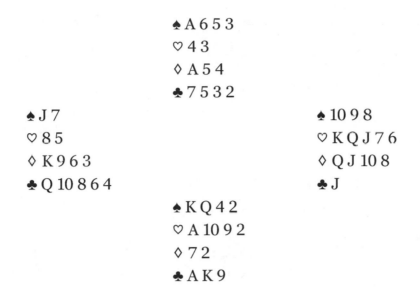

♠A 6 5 3
♥4 3
♦A 5 4
♣7 5 3 2

♠J 7
♥8 5
♦K 9 6 3
♣Q 10 8 6 4

♠10 9 8
♥K Q J 7 6
♦Q J 10 8
♣J

♠K Q 4 2
♥A 10 9 2
♦7 2
♣A K 9

South opened 1NT, 15-18 HCP and reached 4♠ after a Stayman auction. A little pushy by North; maybe he fell in love with his spot cards ☺.

West led the ♥8. Declarer won and played back a heart. When he tried to ruff a heart in dummy, West's spade seven forced dummy's ace. Now East had a trump trick. Declarer lost a trick in every suit. Down one.

Too pushy a contract or was there a way to ten tricks?

In the other room, Trick 1 went ♥8-3-J-A. Declarer tried to take advantage of his ♥109 with a LOL play. He drew the trumps in three rounds ending in the dummy and led a heart. East won the queen and shifted to the ♦Q.

Declarer won the ace and crossed to his hand with a high club. He led the ♥10 and discarded a club from dummy. East won and cashed a diamond, but now declarer had created a club ruff as an extra trick. He cashed the ♥9 pitching another club.

The trade-off of losing an extra heart was profitable. Not only did declarer not lose a club, he also gained a club ruff.

DEAL 127. GETTING THERE, STAYING THERE

                    ♠ 9 3 2
                    ♡ Q 8 3 2
                    ◊ J 8 5 2
                    ♣ Q 10
    ♠ Q 10 6   ♠ J 8 5 4
    ♡ void   ♡ K 7 6 5
    ◊ K 10 4 3   ◊ Q 9 7
    ♣ A K J 8 7 6   ♣ 5 3
                    ♠ A K 7
                    ♡ A J 10 9 4
                    ◊ A 6
                    ♣ 9 4 2

With only East-West vulnerable, South opened 1♡ as dealer and West bid 2♣. North bid 2♡. West doubled 2♡ for takeout. North, knowing his side had nine trumps bid 3♥. That made a clear problem as now the danger of 6-2 clubs could be anticipated.

Declarer was facing two fast club losers and slow losers in diamonds and spades. If he had a trump loser too, ugh. West led the ♣AK and continued the ♣J. Declarer ruffed low and East overruffed, then exited a spade. With no way to reach dummy, declarer lost a spade, a diamond and another trump.

Down two.

If declarer had ruffed with dummy's eight or queen (equals), he would have still lost one trump trick for down only one.

Was there a more successful line of play?

At Trick 3, the declarer in the other room discarded a spade rather than ruff. He was now able to reach dummy with a spade ruff.

First problem solved. To cater to a possible 4-0 trump break, he needed to take care to retain the lead twice in dummy while finessing in trumps.

Had West instead persisted with a fourth round of clubs, declarer could have ruffed in dummy, discarding his losing diamond unless East overruffed.

Making three hearts, losing three clubs and one diamond.

DEAL 128. DOUBLE YOUR PLEASURE

```
                    ♠ A 10 9 7 2
                    ♡ 6 4 3
                    ♢ 9 4
                    ♣ Q 8 7
    ♠ Q J 6 5 4                      ♠ 8
    ♡ 5                              ♡ K Q J 9 8 2
    ♢ K 8 3 2                        ♢ Q J 7 6 5
    ♣ 6 4 3                          ♣ K
                    ♠ K 3
                    ♡ A 10 7
                    ♢ A 10
                    ♣ A J 10 9 5 2
```

South, vulnerable against non-vul opponents, heard the bidding go as follows: Pass – Pass – 4♡ to him. Just great! South ventured 5♣ and everyone passed. West led the ♡5.

South can read East for a red freak. As soon as East's ♠8 falls, South can count 11 tricks setting the ♣7 up by force, discarding first a diamond and then a heart.

Often "Loser On Loser" are nothing more than counting and setting up enough winners instead of trumping cards that can become winners just to avoid losers.

Declarer won the ace. Club finesse? If the club king is with West, he will be out of hearts. He played the club ace and East played the king. OK, spade time before finishing the trumps.

Declarer cashed the spade king, low, low, eight. He led another spade and West played low. Sure, you can see all the hands. But if declarer finessed and lost this trick to East, East would take the setting tricks.

Declarer played the spade ace, East showed out. Declarer led the spade ten and discarded a diamond. LOL # 1. He won the return and went to dummy with a trump. Now the spade nine, discarding a heart. LOL #2. He won the return, finished the trumps and the high spade seven took care of the last heart loser.

A double LOL!

And at the other table?

East opened 1♡ and North-South played in a part score.

Thanks to Larry Cohen for a similar theme from the 2009 Team Trials.

DEAL 129. LOVE THOSE SPOT CARDS!

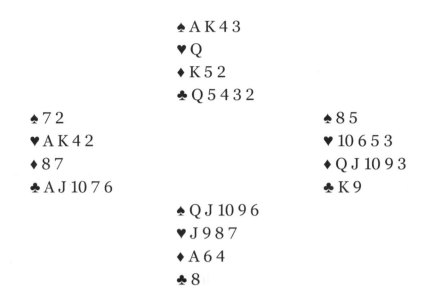

North opened 1♣ as dealer and raised South's 1♠ response to 3♠. South had no trouble continuing to 4♠, but he did have trouble in the play.

West led the ♥A and shifted to the ♠2. He won in hand and ducked a club to East. He won East's trump return in dummy and ruffed a club.

A heart ruff in dummy, another club ruff in hand, and another heart ruff in dummy gave him seven tricks.

But neither dummy's ♣Q nor his own ♥J were high. Two top diamond tricks left him one trick short. Down one.

Was there a tenth trick somewhere?

Yes, a Loser-on-Loser play. At the other table, the auction and start to the play were the same. After winning the trump shift at Trick 2, he led the ♥J for a ruffing finesse through West, who covered with the ♥K.

Declarer ruffed high in dummy, and a second trump to his hand drew the outstanding trumps. Now he ducked the ♥8 to East's ♥10, throwing the ♦2 from dummy, loser on loser, instead of ruffing with dummy's last trump.

This declarer won two top trumps and two top diamonds plus five tricks ruffing. However, he also won a trick with his ♥9, his tenth trick, to make 4♠. Let's hear it for good spot-cards!

DEAL 130. ADDICTED

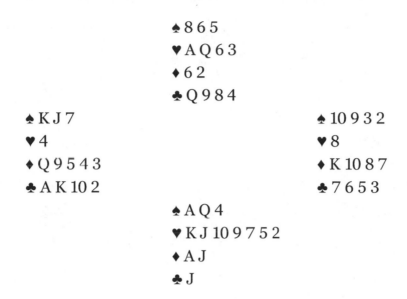

```
                        ♠ 8 6 5
                        ♥ A Q 6 3
                        ♦ 6 2
                        ♣ Q 9 8 4
        ♠ K J 7                         ♠ 10 9 3 2
        ♥ 4                             ♥ 8
        ♦ Q 9 5 4 3                     ♦ K 10 8 7
        ♣ A K 10 2                      ♣ 7 6 5 3
                        ♠ A Q 4
                        ♥ K J 10 9 7 5 2
                        ♦ A J
                        ♣ J
```

South opened 1♥ and West doubled. When North raised hearts, South bid game. West led the ♣A and switched to a low diamond. East's king forced out declarer's ace.

Declarer, a finesse addict, played a trump to dummy and took a spade finesse that was doomed by the bidding.

Down one, losing two spades, one club, and one diamond.

"Partner, you just had those same spot cards on the last hand," moaned North.

How would you have avoided the doomed finesse?

In the other room, declarer wasn't going down without a fight. Trick 1 had removed the club ace and jack, leaving dummy with the ♣Q98. After the same start, at Trick 3 she played a trump to dummy and led the ♣8, discarding her ♦J, LOL # 1.

West won the ♣10 and played another diamond. Declarer ruffed and went to dummy with a trump to lead the ♣9, discarding a spade, LOL # 2.

West won the king, but the defense was finished. The ♣Q for the ♠Q.

Making four hearts, losing three clubs.

DEAL 131. SOME DIAMONDS ARE MERELY CUBIC ZIRCONIA

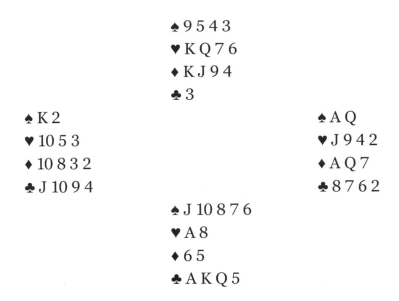

♠ 9 5 4 3
♥ K Q 7 6
♦ K J 9 4
♣ 3

♠ K 2
♥ 10 5 3
♦ 10 8 3 2
♣ J 10 9 4

♠ A Q
♥ J 9 4 2
♦ A Q 7
♣ 8 7 6 2

♠ J 10 8 7 6
♥ A 8
♦ 6 5
♣ A K Q 5

South opened 1♠ and bid 4♠ over her partner's limit raise. West led the ♣J. How to handle the diamonds? Declarer won the ♣A and threw two of dummy's diamonds on her ♣KQ.

Then she cashed the ♥A, ♥K and ♥Q to discard one diamond from her hand. Hoping for a 2-2 trump split, she led the ♠3 from dummy. East won the ♠A and led the ♥J.

Declarer ruffed with the ♠J. West overruffed with the ♠K and shifted to the ♦10. Declarer tried dummy's ♦J. East won the ♦Q, led the ♠Q almost simultaneously and said, "Pair of queens!" That was the setting trick and declarer was down one.

Could declarer have done anything with dummy's diamonds?

Yes. In the other room, the declarer won the ♣A at Trick 1 and didn't bother discarding any diamonds from dummy. He played *four* rounds of hearts from the top to discard *both* of his diamonds, a LOL.

With the 2-2 trump split, the defenders could not separate their trump tricks. Declarer made 4♠, losing one heart and two trump tricks.

DEAL 132. TAKING ADVANTAGE OF A LITTLE SLIP

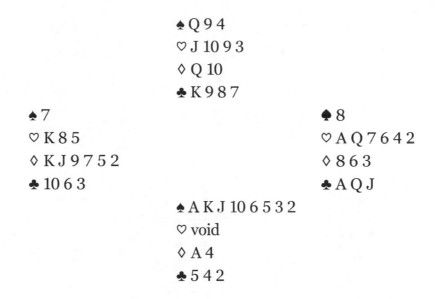

```
                  ♠ Q 9 4
                  ♡ J 10 9 3
                  ◊ Q 10
                  ♣ K 9 8 7
    ♠ 7                           ♠ 8
    ♡ K 8 5                       ♡ A Q 7 6 4 2
    ◊ K J 9 7 5 2                 ◊ 8 6 3
    ♣ 10 6 3                      ♣ A Q J
                  ♠ A K J 10 6 5 3 2
                  ♡ void
                  ◊ A 4
                  ♣ 5 4 2
```

East opened 1♡. South doubled and West bid 2♥. After two passes, South bid 4♠. West led the ♡5, declarer played low, and East played the ace. Declarer ruffed and drew trumps. He tried to set up the clubs, but went down one when West had the diamond king.

Could you have taken advantage of the defensive error?

In the other room, South overcalled 1♠ and both West and North raised their partners. South's 4♠ bid ended the auction. After ruffing the ♡A high at Trick 1, keeping low trumps, he went to dummy in trumps and lead the heart jack. East played low and South discarded a club. West won the heart king and switched to clubs.

Declarer knew East had the heart queen. If West had started with ♡KQ5, he would have led the king. So with the ♡109 in dummy and East holding ◊Qx, declarer could not be prevented from scoring one of dummy's hearts for a diamond discard. Making four spades, losing one heart and two clubs.

What was the defensive error? East was to blame. He knew from the bidding that South was void. At Trick 1, he should have played the heart two, a clear suit preference. The LOL would have failed.

As Porky Pig said "Th-Th-Th-That's all, folks." We hoped you enjoyed this book.

Printed in the United States
by Baker & Taylor Publisher Services